PHILOSOPHICAL APPLICATIONS OF COGNITIVE SCIENCE

PHILOSOPHICAL APPLICATIONS OF COGNITIVE SCIENCE

Alvin I. Goldman
UNIVERSITY OF ARIZONA

Westview Press
BOULDER • SAN FRANCISCO • OXFORD

Focus Series

Published in 1993 in the United States of America by Westview Press, Inc., 5500 Central Avenue, Boulder, Colorado 80301-2877, and in the United Kingdom by Westview Press, 36 Lonsdale Road, Summertown, Oxford OX2 7EW

Library of Congress Cataloging-in-Publication Data
Goldman, Alvin I., 1938–
Philosophical applications of cognitive science / Alvin I. Goldman
p. cm. — (Focus series)
Includes bibliographical references and index.
ISBN 0-8133-8039-1 (cloth). — ISBN 0-8133-8040-5 (pbk.)
1. Philosophy and cognitive science. I. Title. II. Series: Focus series (Westview Press)
B945.G593P55 1993
149—dc20

92-38143
CIP

Printed and bound in the United States of America

The paper used in this publication meets the requirements of the American National Standard for Permanence of Paper for Printed Library Materials Z39.48-1984.

10 9 8 7 6 5 4 3

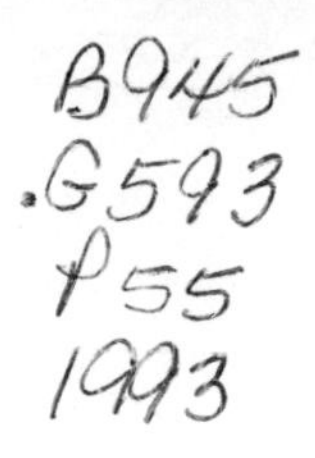

For Raphie and Sidra

Contents

Tables and Figures

Tables

Figures

Preface

The history of philosophy is replete with dissections of the mind, its faculties, and its operations. Historical epistemologists invoked such faculties as the senses, intuition, reason, imagination, and the active and the passive intellect. They wrote of cognitive acts and processes such as judging, conceiving, abstracting, introspecting, synthesizing, and schematizing. Ethicists shared this interest in mental faculties and contents. Moral philosophers studied the appetites, the will, the passions, and the sentiments. All of these philosophers proceeded on the premise that a proper understanding of the mind is essential to many branches of philosophy. This premise is still widely accepted, but time has wrought some changes. In previous centuries the study of the mind was the private preserve of philosophy, and that is no longer true. A number of disciplines have developed a variety of scientific methods, both theoretical and experimental, for studying the mind-brain. These disciplines—the cognitive sciences—include cognitive psychology, developmental psychology, linguistics, artificial intelligence, neuroscience, and cognitive anthropology. Their practitioners attempt to understand and model the mind's wide-ranging activities, such as perception, memory, language processing, inference, choice, and motor control. Philosophy also contributes to the project, but it no longer has a privileged position.

Since it is now clear that the most detailed and reliable information about the mind will emerge from the collective efforts of the cognitive sciences, philosophy should look to those sciences for relevant information and work hand in hand with them. Cognitive science can never *replace* philosophy, since the mission of philosophy extends well beyond the description of mental processes, but it can provide a wide range of helpful fact and theory. In maintaining an alliance with cognitive science, philosophy continues its ancient quest to understand the mind. In the modern age, however, this pursuit requires careful attention to what is being learned by a new group of scientists. Plato and Aristotle created their own physics and cosmologies; contemporary metaphysicians must learn physics and cosmology from physicists. Similarly, while René Descartes and David Hume created their own theories of the mind, contemporary philosophers must give respectful attention to the findings of scientific research.

About 100 years ago, interactions between logic and philosophy assumed dramatic new importance. A similarly dramatic collaboration is now occurring between philosophy and cognitive science. When modern logic emerged in the early years of this century, philosophers saw a powerful new tool that could transform the field. Some believed that philosophy should simply *become* logical analysis, modeled, for example, on Bertrand Russell's theory of descriptions. This was doubtless an excess of zeal. But developments in logic have clearly had wide-ranging and beneficial applications throughout philosophy. Similarly, empirical studies of cognition now have great potential for enriching many areas of philosophy. This book seeks to illustrate and enlarge upon this theme.

This book does not address the methodology of cognitive science: the question of how, in detail, cognitive hypotheses or theories are tested by empirical evidence. Nor does it attempt to *survey* the various cognitive sciences. The bulk of the empirical research presented here is from cognitive psychology, but a bit is drawn from artificial intelligence, linguistics, and neuroscience. I do not attempt to give "equal time" to all of these disciplines or provide a balanced sampling of their theoretical structures. Such samplings are already available in other texts. Rather, the center of attention is the variety of philosophical problems that can benefit from cognitive studies, not the variety of cognitive studies that can contribute to philosophy. At the same time, philosophical morals are often drawn rather briefly, and the instructor or reader will often wish to pursue or debate these morals further.

My selection and discussion of material has been shaped by the desire for a short and accessible text. This constraint has dictated the exclusion of highly technical topics and topics that would require a good deal of groundwork. This is one reason there is rather scant attention to certain important areas of cognitive science, for example, the study of language. Despite such gaps, I hope that the choice of examples conveys the flavor of much of the research in cognitive science as well as its potential fruitfulness for philosophical theory and reflection.

To assist instructors and students in the further exploration of the topics covered here, I have appended a list of suggested readings at the end of each chapter. Many of these readings appear in an anthology I edited entitled *Readings in Philosophy and Cognitive Science* (MIT Press/A Bradford Book, 1993). Conceived partly as a companion to the present text, the anthology contains five chapters that closely parallel this book, plus chapters on language and methodology. I shall abbreviate citations to this anthology by [R]. When [R] follows the citation of a work in a suggested readings section, this indicates that the cited work, or some selection from it (or, occasionally, a closely related work by the same author) appears in the anthology.

I am grateful to a number of people for extremely helpful comments on the first draft of the manuscript: Paul Bloom, Owen Flanagan, Kihyeon Kim, Joseph Tolliver, and Karen Wynn as well as Westview editor Spencer Carr. Their comments resulted in numerous improvements, both substantive and stylistic.

Alvin I. Goldman

Chapter One

Epistemology

The Questions of Epistemology

Epistemology addresses such questions as: (1) What is knowledge? (2) What is rationality? and (3) What are the sources and prospects for human knowledge and rationality? To answer question 3, we would have to inquire into the specific cognitive faculties, processes, or methods that are capable of conferring knowledge or rationality. Cognitive science is clearly relevant to such an inquiry. In asking about the "prospects" for knowledge and rationality, question 3 also hints that there may be limits or failings in people's capacities to know or to be rational. Potential challenges and threats to knowledge and rationality have indeed been a focus of traditional epistemology. Here we shall address threats that stem from the potential inadequacy of some of our cognitive faculties and processes. Thus, whether we are addressing "sources" or "prospects," cognitive science, as the science of our cognitive endowments, can make important contributions to epistemology.

Knowledge and the Sources of Knowledge

Let us start with knowledge, and let us first ask what knowledge consists in. Epistemologists generally agree that knowing, at a minimum, involves having true belief. You cannot know there is a snake under the table unless you believe that there is. Further, you cannot know there is a snake under the table unless it is true, i.e., unless a snake is really there. Epistemologists also agree that mere true belief is not sufficient for knowledge, at least in any strong or robust sense of the term. Suppose you have a phobia for snakes, and you are always imagining them in this or that part of your house. You haven't looked under the table just now, nor has anybody said anything about a snake being there. But you are convinced that a snake is there. On this lone occasion you are right; someone has introduced a harmless garter snake for a practical joke. Is it correct to say that you *know* that a snake is under the table? Surely not. Thus, believing what is true is not enough to claim knowledge.

What must be added to true belief to qualify as knowledge? One popular answer, found in the *reliability* theory of knowledge, says that to be a case of knowing, a true belief must be formed by a cognitive process or method that is generally reliable, i.e., one that generally produces true beliefs. In the snake example this condition is not met. Your supposition that a snake is under the table does not stem from seeing it or from being told about it by someone who has seen it; it results from phobia-driven imagination. This way of forming beliefs is not at all reliable. Hence, although it coincidentally yields true belief on the specific occasion in question, it does not yield knowledge.

A detailed formulation of the reliability theory of knowledge requires many refinements (see Goldman 1979, 1986, 1992b). Let us suppose, however, that something along these general lines is correct. We can then return to the question posed earlier concerning the sources and prospects for human knowledge. Under the reliability theory this question becomes: Which mental faculties and procedures are capable of generating true or accurate beliefs, and which are liable to produce false or inaccurate beliefs?

In the seventeenth and eighteenth centuries, the rationalist and empiricist philosophers debated the question of which faculties were the most reliable for belief formation. The leading empiricists, John Locke, George Berkeley, and David Hume, placed primary emphasis on sense-based learning, whereas rationalists like René Descartes emphasized the superior capacity of reason to generate knowledge. Another central disagreement was over the influence of innate ideas or principles in knowledge acquisition. While the rationalists affirmed the existence of such innate factors, the empiricists denied them.

The debate between Descartes and Berkeley over the nature of depth perception will serve to illustrate this dispute. People regularly form beliefs about the relative distances of objects, but how can such judgments be accurate? What features of vision make such reliable judgment possible? As these early philosophers realized, images formed by light on the retina are essentially two-dimensional arrays. How can such two-dimensional images provide reliable cues to distance or depth?

Descartes (1637) argued that one way people ascertain the distance of objects is by means of the angles formed by straight lines running from the object seen to the eyes of the perceiver. Descartes compared this process to a blind man with a stick in each hand. When he brings the points of the sticks together at the object, he forms a triangle with one hand at each end of the base, and if he knows how far apart his hands are, and what angles the sticks make with his body, he can calculate, "by a kind of geometry *innate* in all men" (emphasis added), how far away the object is. The same geometry applies, Descartes argued, if the observer's eyes are regarded as the ends of the base of a triangle, with the straight lines that extend from them converging at the object, as shown in Figure 1.1. Thus, perceivers can compute the distances of objects by a sort of "natural geometry," knowledge of which is given innately in humankind's divinely endowed reason.

Berkeley, on the other hand, denied that geometric computations enter into the process: "I appeal to anyone's experience whether upon sight of an *object,* he computes its distance by

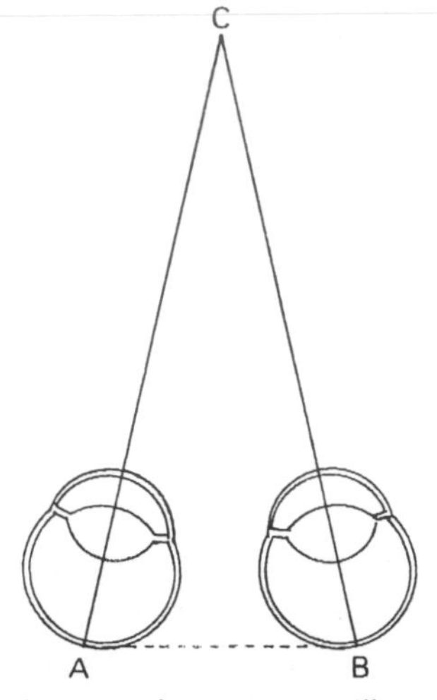

FIGURE 1.1 Schematic drawing (after Descartes) illustrating the distance information provided by convergence. Given the distance between the centers of the two retinas ($\overline{AB}$) and the eyes' angles of regard ($\angle$ CAB and $\angle$CBA), the distance of object C can be computed. *Source:* E. Spelke, "Origins of Visual Knowledge," in D. Osherson, S. Kosslyn, and J. Hollerbach, eds., *Visual Cognition and Action* (Cambridge, Mass.: MIT Press, 1990). Reprinted by permission.

the bigness of the *angle* made by the meeting of the two *optic axes?* ... In vain shall all the mathematicians in the world tell me that I perceive certain lines and angles ... so long as I myself am conscious of no such thing" (1709, sec. 12, italics in original). Berkeley held that distance (or depth) is not immediately perceived by sight but is inferred from past associations between things seen and things touched. Once these past associations are established, the visual sensations are enough to suggest the "tangible" sensations the observer would have if he were near enough to touch the object. Thus, Berkeley's empiricist account of depth perception posits learned associations rather than innate mathematical principles.

This debate about depth perception continues today in contemporary cognitive science, although several new types of cues for depth perception have been proposed. Cognitive scientists also continue to debate the role of innate factors in perception. It is widely thought that perceptual systems have some innately specified "assumptions" about the world that enable them, for the most part, to form accurate representations. An example of such an "assumption" comes from studies of visual motion perception. Wallach and O'Connell (1953) bent pieces of wire into abstract three-dimensional shapes and mounted them in succession on a rotating turntable. They placed a light behind the rotating shape so that it cast a sharp ever-changing shadow on a screen, which was observed by the subject. The shadow was a two-dimensional image varying in time. All other information was removed from sight. Looking at the shadow, however, the subjects perceived the three-dimensional form of the wire shape with no trouble at all. In fact, the perception of three-dimensional form was so strong in this situation that it was impossible for the subjects to perceive the shadow as a rubbery two-dimensional figure. From this and other studies, it has been concluded that the visual system has a built-in "rigidity assumption": Whenever a set of changing two-dimensional elements can be interpreted as a moving rigid body, the visual system interprets it that way. That is, the visual system makes the two-dimensional array *appear* as a rigid, three dimensional body. This response can produce illusions in the laboratory, as when flashing dots on a screen are seen as a smoothly moving rigid body. Presumably, however, the world is largely populated with rigid bodies of which one catches only partial glimpses. So this rigidity assumption produces accurate visual detection *most* of the time. The assumption is innate, and it is pretty reliable.

Visual Object-Recognition

Let us further explore the prospects for vision-based knowledge by considering the way the visual system classifies objects by reference to their shape. And let us ask not simply whether such classification can be reliable, but whether it can be reliable in suboptimal or degraded circumstances, e.g., when one has only a partial glimpse of the object. After all, in everyday life things are not always in full view, and we frequently have to identify them quickly without getting a better view. Under such conditions, can vision still enable us to identify objects correctly as chairs, giraffes, or mushrooms? If so, how does it do this? Classification must ultimately proceed from retinal stimulation. But no unique pattern of retinal stimulation can be associated with a single type of object, nor even a particular instance of the type, since differences in an object's orientation can dramatically affect the retinal image. Furthermore, as just indicated, objects may be partially hidden or occluded behind other surfaces, as when viewed behind foliage. How and when can the visual system still achieve accurate object recognition?

A person stores in memory a large number of representations of various types or categories, such as *chair, giraffe, mushroom,* and so on. When perceiving an object, an observer compares its perceptual representation to the category representations, and when a "match" is found, the perceived object is judged to be an instance of that category. What needs to be explained is (1) how the categories are represented, (2) how the information from the retinal image is processed or transformed, and (3) how this processed information is compared to the stored representations so that the stimulus is assigned to the correct category.

One prominent theory, due to Irving Biederman (1987), begins with the hypothesis that each category of concrete objects is mentally represented as an arrangement of simple volumetric shapes, such as blocks, cylinders, spheres, and wedges. Each of these primitive shapes is called a *geon* (for geometrical ion). Geons can be combined by means of various relations, such as top-of, side-connected, larger-than, and so forth. Each category of objects is represented as a particular combination of related geons. For example, a cup can be represented as a cylindrical geon that is side-connected to a curved, handle-like geon, whereas a pail can be represented by the same two geons but with the handle-like geon on top of the cylindrical geon, as illustrated in Figure 1.2.

The geon theory postulates that when a viewer perceives an object, the visual system interprets the retinal stimulation in terms of geon components and their relations. If the viewer can identify only a few appropriately related geons, he may still be able to uniquely specify the stimulus if only one stored object type has that particular combination of geons. An elephant, for example, may be fully represented by nine component geons, but it may require as few as three geons in appropriate relations to be correctly identified. In other words, even a partial view of an elephant might suffice for accurate recognition if it enables the visual system to recover three geons in suitable relations.

When an object is partially occluded or its contours are somehow degraded, correct identification depends on whether the remaining contours enable the visual system to construct the right geons. Consider Figure 1.3. The left column shows five nondegraded stimulus objects. The middle column has versions of the same objects with some deleted contours. These deleted contours, however, can be reconstructed by the visual system by "filling in" smooth continuous lines. This enables the visual system to recover the relevant geons and identify the objects correctly despite the missing contours. The right column pictures versions of the same objects with different deleted segments. In these versions, the geons cannot be recovered by the visual system because the deletions omit telltale clues of the distinct geons. In the degraded cup, for example, one cannot tell that two geons are present (the bowl part and the handle). This makes identification difficult, if not impossible. Of course, one might

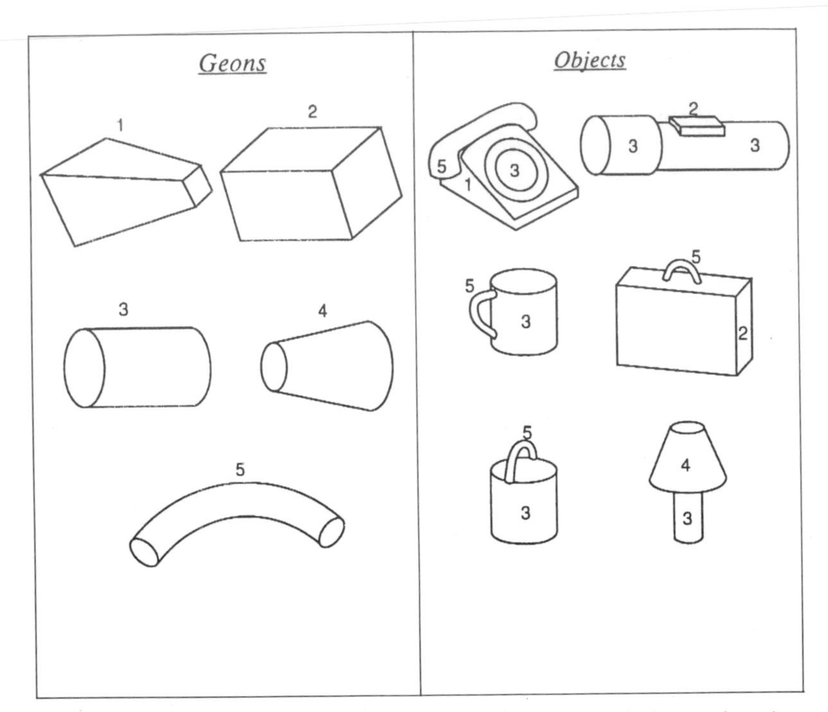

FIGURE 1.2 Geon components and their relations. (Left) A given view of an object can be represented as an arrangement of simple primitive volumes, or geons, of which five are shown here. (Right) Only two or three geons are required to uniquely specify an object. The relations among the geons matter, as illustrated with the pail and cup. *Source:* I. Biederman, "Higher-Level Vision," in D. Osherson, S. Kosslyn, and J. Hollerbach, eds., *Visual Cognition and Action* (Cambridge, Mass.: MIT Press, 1990). Reprinted by permission.

guess rightly that the object is a cup, but such a guess could not yield *knowledge.* There is no *reliable* way of telling that the object is a cup. What Biederman's theory of visual object-recognition reveals is the nature of the reliable process that *does* yield knowledge—a process involving detection of a sufficient number and combination of geons to secure a match to a unique object-model stored in memory. Because of this process, the visual system *can* get enough information to achieve knowledge even when objects are partially hidden or occluded.

The topic of perception is one to which we shall return in Chapter 2, when we discuss theory and observation in science. Right now, however, let us turn to the prospects for human rationality.

Rationality and Evidence

According to one popular principle of rationality, the *total evidence principle,* it is rational for a person S to believe a proposition p at time t only if p is well supported by the total evidence S possesses at t. The intuitive rationale for this requirement is straightforward enough. There are cases in which some of the evidence an agent possesses provides good support for a given proposition, but the support is defeated by other evidence he possesses. For example, upon arriving home from the office, Sam might see his wife's car in the driveway. This supports the proposition that she is home. However, Sam may have additional evidence that undercuts this support. He may know that his wife's car didn't start this morning and that she took a taxi to work instead. Given this total evidence, it would not be rational for Sam to believe that his wife is home.

Granted the plausibility of the total evidence principle, how exactly should we interpret it? What does it mean for a piece of evidence to be *possessed?* Consider an example from Richard Feldman (1988). Suppose my friend Jones tells me that the hike up to Precarious Peak is not terribly strenuous or dangerous, that it is the sort of thing I can do without undue difficulty. Jones knows my abilities with respect to these sorts of things, and he seems to be an honest person. On the basis of his testimony, I believe that the hike is something I can do. Is it rational of me to believe this? Suppose further that I have failed to recall the time Jones told me I could paddle my canoe

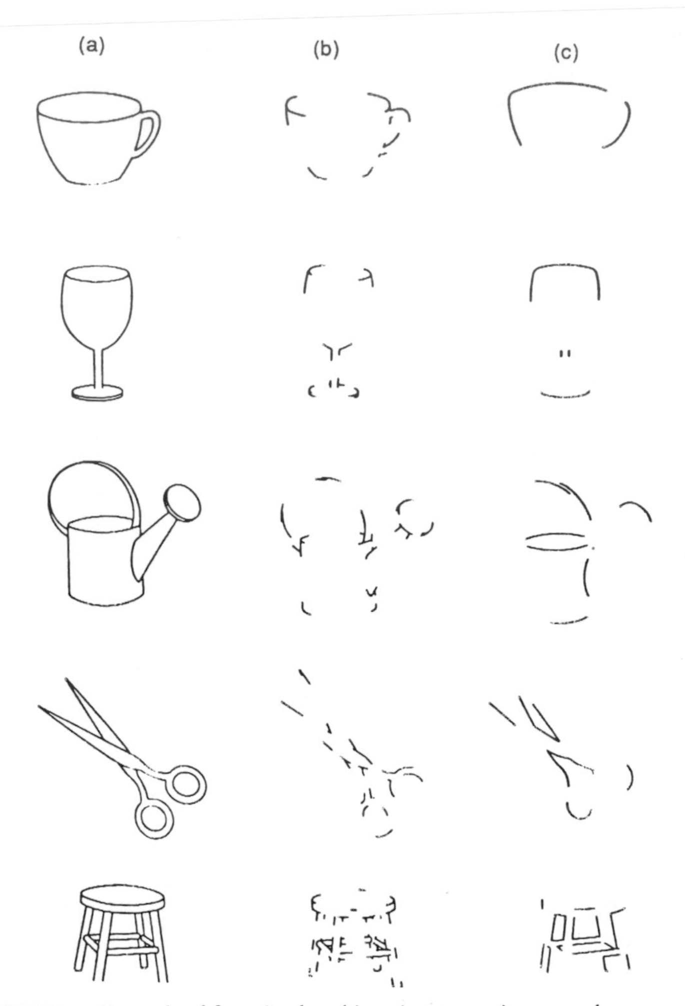

FIGURE 1.3 Example of five stimulus objects in an experiment on the perception of degraded objects. Column (a) shows the original intact versions. Column (b) shows the recoverable versions. Column (c) shows the nonrecoverable versions. *Source:* Modified from I. Biederman, "Human Image Understanding: Recent Experiments and a Theory," *Computer Vision, Graphics, and Image Processing,* 32(1985): 29–73. Reprinted by permission of Academic Press.

down Rapid River, something he knew to be far beyond my abilities, and I don't realize that he just gets a kick out of sending people off on grueling expeditions. Although I fail to recall this incident, it is stored in my memory and I *could* be reminded of it, though in fact nobody does so. Is this unrecalled piece of information a bit of evidence I *possess?* If it isn't part of my "possessed" evidence, then believing that the hike is within my ability is rational for me since I have (other) evidence for trusting Jones. If it *is* part of my possessed evidence, though, then believing that the hike is something I can do is irrational, since this incident undercuts Jones's credibility. The general question suggested by this example is this: When one believes something on the basis of new evidence and fails to recall some bit of counterevidence, when, if ever, does this counterevidence constitute part of the evidence one *possesses?*

Let us compare two answers to this question. One answer is that anything stored in memory is a piece of evidence. A person's total evidence is all the information ever stored in memory and still lodged there, however easy or difficult it may be to retrieve. Clearly, if we accept this answer, it will be easy to fail the demands of rationality. Long-forgotten episodes from childhood that haven't been recalled for twenty or thirty years would qualify as part of one's total evidence; neglect of these episodes, when they are evidentially relevant, would be counted as irrationality.

A second answer posits that an item of evidence is possessed only if it is readily accessible or retrievable from memory. But how accessible is "readily" accessible, and how are degrees of accessibility to be measured? An adequate theory of this subject does not yet exist, but the elements of any such theory obviously should reflect the properties of human memory.

Cognitive psychologists think of memories as varying in strength: the stronger the memory, the greater the probability it will be retrieved and the faster it will be retrieved. Two factors influence strength: (1) decay and (2) interference. As time passes, memory strength gradually lessens through decay. However, reactivation of a memory boosts its strength once more. Only with disuse does it continue to fade or decay. Interference occurs when related or overlapping material becomes mixed with, or substitutes for, the target information. For example, where did you park your car (or bike) when you came to school this morning? This information may be hard to recall because memories of similar episodes of car-parking on other days interfere with your memory of today's parking episode.

Both of these factors, decay and interference, might be at work in the Precarious Peak example. Decay would be partly responsible for my failure to recall that Jones deceived me about canoeing down Rapid River, because it has been a long time since it occurred and I haven't been reminded of it in the meantime. Furthermore, Jones has been perfectly friendly and honest to me on all other matters, so these acts and traits interfere with my memory of the Rapid River episode.

Whether a memory is retrieved on a given occasion depends not only on its strength but also on the retrieval "cues" presented to memory (either deliberately or accidentally). A popular model of memory depicts it as a complex structure of nodes or elements interconnected by means of associative links. When a cue enters memory at one node, it activates that node, and this activation spreads through further portions of the system as a function of the strength of the links between node pairs. The whole process resembles a rumor spreading through a society, where the exact directions and speed of spread depend on the strength of the communicative links between individuals. Whether a given item in memory is retrieved (activated) on a specific occasion depends on what cues enter the system and on the prior associations, or associative pathways, between the cued node(s) and the target node. A target node will be difficult to retrieve from a given starting point (say, the thought of proposition p) if it is unlikely that a strong pathway will emerge. For example, if you start with the goal of activating an image of your third-grade teacher, there may be few cues that would achieve this result. But if someone reminded you of a dramatic incident involving the teacher, that cue might suffice.

These complexities dim the hopes of getting any simple measure of "ready accessibility," and hence any simple measure of evidence "possession." Perhaps the moral to be drawn is that simple principles appealing to the notion of "possession" should be abandoned in favor of more complex and subtle principles. Any detailed principle of rationality must recognize that human belief formation operates under the constraints of memory and must take the psychology of memory into account.

Self-Deception and Memory

It is widely noticed that people tend to have unrealistically inflated opinions of themselves. Although this is something of a commonplace, it is interesting to find experimental support for it in psychology. Moreover, it is not entirely obvious just what is the source of such illusions. Exactly which processes initiate and maintain these opinions? This question can only be answered by cognitive science.

Summarizing a variety of research, Shelley Taylor (1989) reports that illusions about the self are particularly prevalent among children. Children believe that they are capable of many tasks, including ones they have never tried. Most kindergartners and first-graders say they are at or near the top of the class. They have great expectations for their future success. Moreover, these grandiose assessments are quite unresponsive to negative feedback, at least until about age seven. It is Taylor's thesis that such illusions contribute quite positively to mental health. From an epistemological point of view, however, they certainly smack of irrationality.

There is considerable evidence that positive self-illusions are also prevalent among adults. Most people, for example, see themselves as better than others and as above average in most of their qualities. Because it is logically impossible for most people to be better than everyone else, this positive view of themselves appears to be, at least to some degree, illusory or nonveridical. In one survey, 90 percent of automobile drivers considered themselves to be better than average drivers. Obviously, only about half of these people can be right. People whose driving had involved them in accidents serious enough to involve hospitalization and drivers with no accident histories gave almost identical descriptions of their driving abilities. Irrespective of their accident records, people judged themselves to be more skillful than average.

One psychological explanation of these findings might invoke the notion of *self-schemas:* mental structures that guide the selection and retrieval of information about the self. A dinner guest who thinks of himself as witty is likely to interpret his barbed remark toward another guest as humorous and is likely to recall this witticism later (even if other guests did not find the remark witty at all). In recalling information that fits a self-schema, he inadvertently reinforces the self-schema. Each situation that the witty person interprets as an example of his witty banter provides him with additional evidence that he is witty. Thus, a self-schema both enables us to interpret the information that fits our prior conception of ourselves and helps cement that self-conception.

One problem here is that our prior theory about the self appears to influence our perception of the evidence. This is a topic we shall discuss in Chapter 2. A second problem is that memory seems to retrieve instances that lend positive support to the theory. The self-styled witty person more easily retrieves his witticisms than his attempts at witticism that fell perceptibly flat. Let us focus on the second problem. If this selection process is indeed a feature of memory, it would seem to constitute an irrational bias. If positive pieces of evidence are better stored in memory or more likely to be recalled than negative pieces, then there can be no fair weighing of the total evidence one has accumulated.

Although this general hypothesis has not been fully explored by cognitive psychologists, it poses questions concerning the very structure of memory sketched earlier. Pairs of nodes in memory may be linked more readily if their contents *cohere,* or fit with one another, and positive instances of a trait would be one example of coherence. If this is correct, then when an accepted contention is queried, it will be easier for memory to recall positive support for that contention than negative evidence, even if the latter has been plentiful.

A somewhat different approach to the phenomenon of self-illusion emphasizes the role of wishful thinking. Young children, for example, do not differentiate very well between what they wish were true and what they think is true, and this trait could account for their estimations of their abilities (Stipek 1984). Wishful thinking and other desire-infected cognitions may also be important in adults and may drive the processes of memory. Anthony Greenwald (1980) suggests that memory often fabricates and revises our personal history. Unlike the academic historian, who is expected to adhere closely to the facts and insert a personal evaluation only in the interpretation, the personal historian takes unbridled license with the facts themselves, rearranging and distorting them and omitting aspects of history altogether in an effort to create and maintain a favorable image of the self. As writer Carlos Fuentes observes, "Desire will send you back into memory ... for memory is desire satisfied." (Fuentes 1964, 58).

Taylor surveys many other cognitive mechanisms and strategies by which people unrealistically enhance their self-image or their assessment of their situation and prospects in life. It seems clear, then, that at least on the topic of the *self,* people have tendencies toward *epistemic irrationality,* as philosophers call it, where the "epistemic" dimension is concerned with the pursuit of objective truth. These tendencies may be rational in a prudential or pragmatic sense; indeed, research evidence indicates that self-enhancing strategies lead to higher motivation, greater persistence at tasks, more effective performance, and greater success. From the standpoint of truth or accuracy, however, they leave much to be desired.

Logic and Rationality

Let us move from questions of memory to other dimensions of people's capacities to be (epistemically) rational. It is widely agreed that rational belief depends on the logical and probabilistic relations that hold between hypotheses and evidence. For a belief to be rational, it must either follow *logically* from the evidence or be highly *probable* on that evidence. The prospects for rational belief, then, depend heavily on people's abilities to detect logical and probabilistic relations among propositions. Just how strong are people's abilities in these respects? In particular, how proficient are untutored thinkers at logic and probability tasks? While the answers are not all in, these are questions to which cognitive scientists have devoted a good bit of attention.

Starting with human competence at logic, let us first consider a study (Rips and Marcus 1977) in which subjects were asked to judge the validity of simple argument forms involving a conditional (if-then) sentence. Four of these arguments were: Modus Ponens (If P then Q; P; therefore Q); Modus Tollens (If P then Q; not-Q; therefore not-P); Affirming the Consequent (If P then Q; Q; therefore P); and Denying the Antecedent (If P then Q; not-P; therefore not-Q). The first two of these, of course, are valid, and the second two are invalid. One hundred percent of the subjects marked Modus Ponens valid, which of course is good news for defenders of human logical competence. But only 57 percent judged Modus Tollens to be valid. Even worse is the fact that 23 percent of the subjects wrongly judged Affirming the Consequent to be valid and 21 percent judged Denying the Antecedent to be valid. These results, however, are not wholly conclusive. Some researchers point out that people commonly misunderstand English conditional sentences, often because they interpret them as biconditionals ("if and only if" statements). If this was the interpretation of the subjects who marked Affirming the Consequent or Denying the Antecedent valid, they were not guilty of a fallacy, just a linguistic misunderstanding. In any case, let us examine some other studies and their implications.

Lance Rips (1989) used puzzles about knights and knaves to study people's logic competences. One puzzle, drawn from Smullyan (1978), begins like this. Suppose there is an island where there are just two sorts of inhabitants—knights, who always tell the truth, and knaves, who always lie. Nothing distinguishes knights and knaves but their lying or truth-telling propensities. You overhear a conversation between two or more inhabitants and on the basis of this conversation you must decide which of the individuals are knights and which are knaves. For example, we have three inhabitants, A, B, and C, each of whom is a knight or a knave. Two people are said to be of the same type if they are both knights or both knaves. A and B make the following statements:

A: B is a knave.
B: A and C are of the same type.

What is C?

Here is how this problem can be solved. Suppose that A is a

knight. Since what he says is true, B would then be a knave. But if B is a knave, he is lying, which means that A and C are not of the same type. We're assuming that A is a knight; so on this assumption, C must be a knave. But what if A is a knave rather than a knight? In that case, A's statement is false, and hence B is a knight and his statement is true. This makes A and C of the same type, which means that C is a knave. So no matter whether we take A to be a knight or a knave, C will be a knave, and this must be the answer to the puzzle.

I have just told you how to solve this problem. But how well do untutored people perform when left to themselves? Problems of this kind were given to undergraduates who had never taken a formal course in logic. Some subjects did quite well. Rips quotes a transcript (or protocol) of the tape-recorded remarks of one of the most articulate subjects as she worked on this puzzle, and her remarks come close to duplicating the reasoning presented above. Unfortunately, this subject was not very typical. In all there were thirty-four subjects in the study. Ten of these stopped working the problems within fifteen minutes after beginning the test, and these ten solved only 2.5 percent of the problems. For the group as a whole, the solution rate was only 20 percent. The least successful subject got 0 percent correct and the most successful subject got 84 percent correct.

Rips's own theory about human logical competence is quite optimistic. He postulates that people have, as part of their primitive psychological equipment, rules of inference that correspond to rules in formal systems (so-called "natural deduction systems"). These rules include the following: And = Elimination (P and Q entails P); Modus Ponens (If P then Q and P jointly entail Q); De Morgan's Law (Not [P or Q] entails Not P and Not Q); and Disjunctive Syllogism (P or Q and Not P jointly entail Q). Of course, mere possession of such rules is not enough. To solve these puzzles, the rules must be applied to the premises given in each puzzle and then used repeatedly and systematically to obtain intermediate results and then final results. The set of guidelines for applying such rules may be called a *control system* or a set of *inference strategies.* Rips constructed a computer program in PROLOG incorporating such strategies, and it solves thirty-three of the knight-knave puzzles given to the group of experimental subjects.

If people have the same inference rules as Rips's program, why is their performance so inferior? One possibility is that they have a memory deficiency rather than a strictly logical deficiency. They may forget the intermediate results obtained in earlier steps of their reasoning (although the subjects in the reported experiment were allowed to write things down). Second, they may not have a satisfactory system of "conceptual bookkeeping." That is, they may lack a systematic method of listing the possible ways in which A, B, and C can be assigned to the knight/knave categories. Third, they may not have a systematic set of strategies for "chaining through" all the possibilities. Precisely this is suggested by one pair of commentators, Johnson-Laird and Byrne (1990). They claim that untutored people do not have systematic strategies built into their "logical architecture." People can devise strategies after experience with the puzzles, but these are generally simple and limited strategies rather than systematic, thoroughgoing, or "effective" ones.

Notice that these hypotheses are compatible with Rips's postulate that people have natural-deduction-style inference rules as part of their logical equipment. Taken together, these theories leave open a prospect for moderate optimism, viz., that people do possess correct inference rules but are lacking in effective strategies or control structures.

It is premature, however, to place much confidence in this hypothesis. Almost all of the experimental studies have been done on young adults, and although these subjects have not taken formal courses in logic, they may well have been exposed in their education or culture to specimens of rigorous logical reasoning. Deductive argumentation, for example, appears in high school geometry classes, elsewhere in formal education, in selected conversation, and in literature. A moderately literate person encounters logic-like reasoning in many contexts. Perhaps subjects' performance on the knight-knave puzzles reflects their ability to "model" reasoning patterns to which they have been exposed rather than revealing any "hard-wired" logical inference rules. Thus, a clear picture of people's innate logical competence has yet to emerge.

More theoretical reflections on people's abilities at logic tasks shed light on the sorts of requirements on rationality that epistemologists have commonly suggested. Epistemologists often say that a rational set of beliefs must be *logically consistent,* i.e., beliefs that do not jointly entail any contradiction. This sort of demand is especially associated with the *coherence* theory (see Chapter 2). Since consistency is the mere absence of contradiction, one might suppose that it would be easy to achieve and that this much should be within the capacities of human reasoners. In fact, the consistency condition is extremely difficult to satisfy in any systematic and timely fashion, as Christopher Cherniak (1986) has pointed out.

Let us confine our attention to truth-functional consistency, the consistency of propositions involving their truth-functional connectives, such as "not," "and," "or" and "if-then." Three propositions of the form "If P then Q," "P, " and "Not-Q" are truth-functionally inconsistent because their truth-functional structures imply that they cannot be jointly true. A *truth table* lists all the logically possible truth-value assignments to the several propositions. In Table 1.1, we suppose that "If P then Q," "P, " and "Not-Q" represent the three believed propositions. Each row constitutes one possible set of truth-value assignments to the atomic propositions, P and Q, where "T" represents truth and "F" represents falsity. To ask whether the three believed propositions are consistent is to ask whether it is logically possible that all three of these propositions could be true together; that is, whether it is logically possible that their conjunction could be true. Thus, we record their conjunction in the final column of the table and see whether it turns out true under any possible truth-value assignment. If there are all F's in this column, then the three components are jointly inconsistent. If there is at least one T, then the component propositions are consistent. As Table 1.1 shows, these propositions are inconsistent.

If a person wished to check his beliefs for truth-functional consistency, truth tables would be one systematic ("effective") way of doing so. And it looks pretty simple. But how many rows need to be checked? The number of rows is determined by the number of possible truth-value assignments to the atomic propositions. If n is the number of logically independent atomic propositions involved (2 in our example: P and Q), the number of possible assignments is 2^n. Thus, if the number of independent propositions is 4, the number of rows is 16; if the number of independent propositions is 8, the number of rows is 256. As one can see, 2^n grows very rapidly as n increases. In fact, if $n = 138$, 2^n is approximately 3.5×10^{41}. This is a very large number of rows that would have to be checked in order to determine the consistency of a system of beliefs with 138 independent atomic propositions, a rather modest-sized belief system. How long would it take to check a truth table with that many rows? Cherniak has calculated that if an ideal computer worked at "top speed," and could check each row in the time it takes a light ray to traverse the diameter of a proton, it would still take twenty billion years! Obviously this task is infeasible within any reasonable time even for an ideal computer, and it is many orders of magnitude beyond the feasibility of human beings. Thus, while consistency may be an epistemic ideal, it is well beyond our capacity to guarantee conformity with this ideal.

TABLE 1.1 Logically Possible Truth-Value Assignments to Several Propositions

P	*Q*	*If P then Q*	*Not-Q*	*(If P then Q) & (P) & (Not-Q)*
T	T	T	F	F
T	F	F	T	F
F	T	T	F	F
F	F	T	T	F

What should we conclude from this about the prospects for human rationality? The pessimistic conclusion that our prospects for rationality are not that good assumes that consistency is indeed a sine qua non of rationality. An alternative is to rethink and revise our theory of rationality. Perhaps a human being who fails to notice an inconsistency in his belief-set is not ipso facto irrational. At any rate, there would seem to be *some* notion of rationality—perhaps it should be called *reasonability*—that is sensitive to practical possibilities or computational feasibilities. Since systematic checks for consistency are infeasible, it is not unreasonable of an agent to refrain from trying to execute such a check, and hence it is not necessarily unreasonable for such an agent to fall into inconsistency. Even famous logicians like Gottlob Frege proposed systems of axioms that proved to be inconsistent. Requirements of rationality, then, should be shaped to fit practical feasibilities, and questions of feasibility are just the sorts of questions which cognitive science often addresses. Thus, cognitive science may be relevant in setting standards for rationality, not just in assessing human prospects for meeting independently given standards.

Probability and Rationality

Since evidential support involves not only logical but probabilistic relations, we turn next to human prospects for detecting the latter. People seem to have at least a minimal grasp of probabilistic matters. For example, undergraduate subjects have been given the following three-card problem (Osherson 1990; Bar-Hillel and Falk 1982):

> Three cards are in a hat. One is red on both sides (the red-red card). One is white on both sides (the white-white card). One is red on one side and white on the other (the red-white card). A single card is drawn randomly and tossed into the air.
>
> a. What is the probability that the red-red card was drawn?
> b. What is the probability that the drawn card lands with a white side up?
> c. What is the probability that the red-red card was drawn, assuming that the drawn card lands with a red side up? (Osherson 1990, 56)

Most subjects gave correct answers to questions a and b, though a wrong answer to question c. (The correct answers are $^1/_3$, $^1/_2$, and $^2/_3$, respectively.)

Consider now another set of probability problems posed to subjects by Daniel Kahneman and Amos Tversky. Subjects were first given the following instructions:

> A panel of psychologists have interviewed and administered personality tests to 30 engineers and 70 lawyers. On the basis of this information, thumbnail descriptions of the 30 engineers and 70 lawyers have been written. You will find on your forms five descriptions, chosen at random from the 100 available descriptions. For each description, please indicate your probability that the person described is an engineer, on a scale from 0 to 100 (Kahneman and Tversky 1973, 241).

The subjects who read these instructions will be called the "low engineer group." A different group of subjects was given identical instructions except that the numbers 70 and 30 were reversed: They were told that there were 70 engineers and 30 lawyers. This will be called the "high engineer group."

Subjects in both groups were presented with the same descriptions, such as the following:

> Jack is a 45-year-old man. He is married and has four children. He is generally conservative, careful, and ambitious. He shows no interest in political and social issues and spends most of his free time on his many hobbies, which include home carpentry, sailing, and mathematical puzzles.
>
> The probability that Jack is one of the 30 engineers [or 70 engineers, for the high engineer group] in the sample of 100 is ____ percent (Kahneman and Tversky 1973, 241).

Following the five descriptions, the subjects encountered the *null* description:

> Suppose now that you were given no information whatsoever about an individual chosen at random from the sample.
>
> The probability that this man is one of the 30 engineers in the sample of 100 is ____ percent (Kahneman and Tversky 1973, 241).

How would proper probabilistic reasoning instruct the subjects to respond to these tasks of assigning probabilities? Although there is some controversy on this matter, let us follow the dominant view that proper probabilistic reasoning is "Bayesian" reasoning, which would require subjects to take into account the *prior odds* of someone's being an engineer in advance of any specific information about him. These prior odds should reflect the "base rate" information, either the 30/70 ratio of engineers to lawyers given to the low engineer group or the 70/30 ratio given to the high engineer group.

When subjects were given the null description, their answers clearly used the prior odds. The low engineer group assigned a probability of 30 percent to an individual's being an engineer and the high engineer group assigned a probability of 70 percent. Elsewhere, however, both groups tended to ignore the base rates.

Consider what would happen if principles of Bayesian probability were used in this experiment. Assume that the two groups assigned, on average, the same value to the probability that Jack's characteristics would be those of an engineer. (The number of engineers in the sample does not affect this probability.) Then if the two groups made proper use of the base rate information, or prior odds, the ratio of their average answers would be .3/.7 or .43. In fact, the obtained ratio was very close to 1. In other words, the low and high engineer groups offered essentially identical estimates. Clearly, their calculations completely neglected the base rates.

As a further test of this phenomenon, Kahneman and Tversky constructed the following description, designed so as to be uninformative about the protagonist's profession:

> Dick is a 30-year-old man. He is married with no children. A man of high ability and high motivation, he promises to be quite successful in his field. He is well liked by his colleagues (Kahneman and Tversky 1973, 242).

Both groups judged the probability that Dick is an engineer about the same, i.e., around 50 percent. Again they responded solely to the description—in this case its inconclusiveness—while neglecting the base rate information. In these types of cases, then, people tend to demonstrate a rather poor grasp of probabilistic principles.

A similar assessment emerges from another experiment by the same researchers. Tversky and Kahneman gave subjects the following problem:

> Linda is 31 years old, single, outspoken, and very bright. She majored in philosophy. As a student, she was deeply concerned with issues of discrimination and social justice, and also participated in antinuclear demonstrations.
>
> Please rank the following statements by their probability, using 1 for the most probable and 6 for the least probable.

a. Linda is a teacher in elementary school.
b. Linda works in a bookstore and takes yoga classes.
c. Linda is active in the feminist movement.
d. Linda is a psychiatric social worker.
e. Linda is a member of the League of Women Voters.
f. Linda is a bank teller.
g. Linda is an insurance salesperson.
h. Linda is a bank teller and is active in the feminist movement (Tversky and Kahneman 1983, 296).

Almost 90 percent of the subjects ranked (h) as more probable than (f). Notice that (h) is a conjunction and (f) is one of its conjuncts. It is an axiom of the standard probability calculus, however, that no conjunction can be more probable than one of its conjuncts. For example, how could the probability that it will *both* rain and be windy tomorrow be greater than the probability that it will rain tomorrow? Every possible situation in which it both rains and blows is also a situation in which it rains; but there can be situations in which it rains and doesn't blow (much). So rain must be at least as probable as rain and wind; the latter cannot be more probable than the former. To judge the probability of the conjunction higher than that of a conjunct, therefore, is to commit the *conjunction fallacy.* Although the subjects in the original study had no background in probability or statistics, roughly the same 90 percent fallacy rate was obtained on this problem for graduate and professional students who had taken one or more courses in statistics, and a very high rate was also obtained for doctoral students in a decision science program.

Tversky and Kahneman hypothesize that these and other violations of the probability calculus result from the use of a primitive psychological heuristic that they call the *representativeness heuristic.* The representativeness heuristic is the tendency to judge the probability that an object x belongs in category C by the degree to which x is representative of, or similar to, typical members of category C. For example, given a description of Dick that sounds equally similar to an engineer and a lawyer, people tend to judge the probability of Dick's being an engineer to be 50 percent. When offered the alternative of Linda being a bank teller, they judge the probability to be low because Linda is not very similar to a typical bank teller. Linda is more similar, however, to a typical member of the category containing feminist bank tellers. Thus, the probability of this alternative is judged to be higher than the probability of her just being a bank teller.

The power of the representativeness heuristic was further illustrated by a study devised to see if subjects would recognize the validity of the conjunction rule even if they did not apply it spontaneously. Subjects were asked to indicate which of the following two arguments they found more convincing:

> Argument 1. Linda is more likely to be a bank teller than she is to be a feminist bank teller, because every feminist bank teller is a bank teller, but some women bank tellers are not feminists, and Linda could be one of them.
>
> Argument 2. Linda is more likely to be a feminist bank teller than she is likely to be a bank teller, because she resembles an active feminist more than she resembles a bank teller (Tversky and Kahneman 1983, 299).

Sixty-five percent of the subjects chose the resemblance argument, Argument 2, over the conjunction rule argument, Argument 1. Thus, even a deliberate attempt to induce a reflective attitude did not eliminate the appeal of the representativeness heuristic.

These studies give strong support to the idea that people's understanding of probability is very weak. Not only do people fail to use or even recognize basic principles like the conjunction rule, but they also have other operations in place that produce conflict with the conjunction rule for a certain class of examples.

More recent experiments, however, paint a more optimistic picture of human performance in probability judgment. Focusing primarily on the matter of base-rate neglect, Gerd Gigerenzer and his collaborators (Gigerenzer, Hell, and Blank, 1988) found that when they called attention to appropriate information, base-rate neglect was greatly reduced and even disappeared. They also found that subjects do not use representativeness as a general, all-purpose heuristic in probability judgment. Gigerenzer et al. first did a variation of Kahneman and Tversky's engineer-lawyer experiment. A typical subject was shown 10 sheets of paper, three marked with an "E" for engineer and seven marked with an "L" for lawyer. The experimenter folded the sheets, threw them into an empty urn, and shook them. After observing a random drawing of one of the descriptions from the urn, the subject judged the probability that the person described was an engineer. When random sampling was thus visually observed, probability judgments were closer to Bayesian predictions than to the predictions dictated by the representativeness heuristic.

In another experiment, Gigerenzer et al. selected a problem in probability revision that is familiar from everyday life and where varying base rates is very natural. Spectators watching league soccer games encounter probability revision problems all the time. Before a game they have some expectation about the probability that Team A will win based on that team's win-loss record. This is base-rate information. During the game, they get new diagnostic information, e.g., that Team A is two goals behind at halftime. The task of revising their probability estimates in light of this new information has the same structure as the engineer-lawyer problem. If simple representativeness were a general-purpose heuristic of the brain, subjects tested on such tasks would use only the half-time score to predict the final outcome. They would ignore the team's record, i.e., the base rate. In fact, there was no base-rate neglect in an experimental test with the soccer problem. The vast majority of subjects reported using strategies relying in part on base rates; almost all approached some version (qualitative, not quantitative) of Bayesian inference.

Similarly, subjects can sometimes be brought to appreciate the significance of conjunctiveness, or nesting, among events. One group of Tversky and Kahneman's subjects was asked to consider a regular six-sided die with four green faces and two red faces. The die would be rolled twenty times and the sequence of greens (G) and reds (R) would be recorded. The subjects were then asked to choose one of the two sequences below, with the prospect of winning $25 if the chosen sequence appeared on successive rolls of the die.

1. RGRRR
2. GRGRRR

Subjects were also given two arguments, one in favor of choosing the first sequence and the other in favor of the second:

> Argument 1: The first sequence is more probable than the second because the second sequence is the same as the first with an additional G at the beginning. Hence, every time the second sequence occurs, the first sequence must also occur. Consequently, you can win on the first and lose on the second, but you can never win on the second and lose on the first.
>
> Argument 2: The second sequence is more probable than the first because the proportions of R and G in the second sequence are closer than those of the first sequence to the expected proportions of R and G for a die with four green and two red faces (Tversky and Kahneman 1983, 304).

Most of the subjects (76 percent) chose the first argument, which expresses the gist of the conjunction rule, over the second, which describes the line of thinking under the representativeness heuristic. These formulations enabled untutored subjects to appreciate the force of the conjunction rule. In a similar vein, Richard Nisbett et al. (1983) provided evidence that correct probabilistic reasoning is encouraged by emphasizing the role of chance in producing the events in question and by clarifying the sample space and the sampling process.

Until now we have assumed that a necessary condition of rationality is conformity with the probability calculus—that if people fail to conform their judgments to the principles of probability, then they aren't rational. This assumption, however, is open to question. Undoubtedly it is intellectually desirable to conform one's beliefs to correct principles of probability. But is the absence of such principles in one's basic cognitive equipment a mark of irrationality? The answer depends on exactly how we conceive the standard of rationality. Does rationality require fundamental cognitive faculties to be "hard-wired" with all desirable intellectual principles? Or might it suffice for these faculties to have the capacity to learn all such principles? Let us call these alternatives, respectively, the *innate possession* conception of rationality and the *learnability* conception of rationality.

One illustration of the latter concerns memory strategies. There are useful mnemonic principles that people can eventually learn but that do not come hard-wired. One such strategy is clustering, or "chunking." Suppose someone asks you to remember the following list and tells you that you may repeat it back in any order you like: *table, dog, spoon, chair, cat, fork, lamp, bird, knife, rug, pig, plate.* Even if you heard this list only once, it wouldn't be hard to recall all the items. You would notice the obvious structure in the list and organize your memory into the categories of "furniture," "dining implements," and "animals." This procedure must be learned; young children don't use it. Although it would be a nice design feature for humans to come equipped with prior knowledge of how to deploy memory (or metamemory), we apparently do not. But is this a flaw in our cognitive equipment?

Our failure to come equipped with metamemorial knowledge or with the principles of probability is not necessarily a flaw in rationality as long as we have the capacity to learn such principles.

These studies all indicate that cognitive science can contribute to epistemology in two ways. First, it can address the prospects for human knowledge and rational belief by surveying our native endowments in various domains, including perception, deductive reasoning, and probabilistic reasoning. Second, it can help *set* the standards for rationality—for example, by spelling out the options of what might count as evidence possession, or by giving us a realistic perspective on whether to impose an innate possession conception of rationality or some weaker requirement, such as the learnability conception.

Suggestions for Further Reading

On the reliability approach to knowledge and justified belief, see Dretske (1981), Goldman (1986), and Goldman (1992a Part 2) [R]. ([R] following a citation indicates that the cited work, or some selection from it, or a closely related work by the same author, appears in Goldman 1993b.)

The topic of visual perception is usefully approached through Spelke (1990a) and Biederman (1990) [R]. Marr (1982) is a classic though difficult work.

On memory and rationality, see Potter (1990), Feldman (1988), Goldman (1986, chap. 10), and Cherniak (1986, chap. 3).

Some major psychological approaches to deductive reasoning are presented in Holland et al. (1986, sections 9.2 and 9.3) [R], Rips (1989), and Johnson-Laird and Byrne (1991). A more philosophical discussion of deduction and rationality is Cherniak (1986, chap. 4).

Many influential articles on probability judgment appear in Kahneman, Slovic, and Tversky (1982) [R]. A one-chapter survey and analysis is Osherson (1990). For philosophical debate on the relevance of empirical research to human rationality, see Cohen (1981) and Stich (1990). A pessimistic assessment of human inferential competence appears in Nisbett and Ross (1980); more optimistic perspectives appear in Gigerenzer et al. (1988) and Kornblith (1993) [R].

Chapter Two

Philosophy of Science

Is Observation Theory-Laden?

The philosophy of science, a branch of epistemology, studies the nature of scientific knowledge and understanding. For much of this century, philosophy of science emphasized the "logic" of science in abstraction from, and often in direct opposition to, the psychology of actual scientists. Currently, however, there are attempts to study the mental processes crucial to scientific thought and inquiry. This endeavor may be called *the cognitive science of science,* with "science" construed broadly to include mathematics (a so-called "formal" science) as well as the empirical sciences.

A hallmark of empirical science, it is often said, is that the choice between scientific hypotheses or theories can be adjudicated by empirical test. In observing the results of experiments, scientists may decide to retain theories borne out by the observations while abandoning those that conflict with the evidence. Such confrontations with observable fact seem crucial to the objectivity of science.

There are many problems concerning the choice of scientific theories; one such problem is observation itself. In the traditional picture of observation, a scientist is able to tell "directly" whether a certain experimental outcome did or did not occur. Detection of the outcome does not depend on any other beliefs of the scientist; specifically, its occurrence or nonoccurrence can be determined independently of which theory the scientist already accepts or is prone to accept. Such a separation of observation and theoretical preconception seems crucial to an objective test of competing theories. If an experimental result appears one way to a scientist who accepts one theory but a different way to a scientist who accepts a competing theory, then observation has failed to provide a method for choosing between the theories or for settling disputes about the nature of the world. Such cases suffer from a kind of circularity. Thus, scientific objectivity seems to require the *theory independence*, or *theory neutrality,* of observation.

In traditional discussions of theory and observation, it was assumed that observation satisfied this requirement. But this assumption involves tacit appeal to a premise, viz., that the psychological processes of observation do not draw on the theoretical beliefs of the observing scientist. In the late 1950s and early 1960s, however, some philosophers of science challenged this assumption. Based partly on the New Look movement in psychology, philosophers and historians such as N. R. Hanson and Thomas Kuhn denied the assumption of theory neutrality. Instead, they claimed that observation is *laden with theory.* The very observations of a scientist are infected by what he or she already believes. This poses a serious challenge to the objectivity of science.

Hanson (1958) asked us to imagine Johannes Kepler and Tycho Brahe watching the dawn. Noting that Kepler regarded the sun as fixed, with the earth moving around it, whereas Brahe viewed the earth as being fixed with the sun revolving around it, Hanson asked whether Kepler and Brahe would really see the same thing and concluded that they would not. He compared this case to that of seeing reversible figures, e.g., a drawing that can be seen as a duck or a rabbit, or one that resembles both an antelope and a bird. When looking at such drawings, we notice that the perceptual appearance can reverse. Hanson followed the Gestalt and New Look psychologists in holding that what one sees is a function of one's "set" or expectations; it reflects how prior experience or training have prepared the visual system for its encounters with the world. If a trained physicist and an Eskimo baby were both shown an X-ray tube, they would not "see the same thing" (at least in one sense of that expression).

Kuhn (1962) developed these themes further. He claimed that a theoretical outlook, or conceptual scheme, which he called a *paradigm,* is prerequisite to perception itself. A change in paradigm causes a scientist to experience the world of his research-engagements differently, as in a Gestalt switch. Similar themes have been advanced by Nelson Goodman: "That we find what we are prepared to find (what we look for or what forcefully affronts our expectations), and that we are likely to be blind to what neither helps nor hinders our pursuits, are commonplaces ... amply attested in the psychological laboratory" (Goodman 1978, 14).

Are these claims about the theory-laden quality of perception borne out by continued psychological research? Jerry Fodor, for one, disputes this conclusion. Although Fodor admits that something like a "background theory" is used by perceptual systems, he claims that these systems are not influenced by the sort of theory one learns as a scientist. Fodor (1984) posits that perceptual systems are *modular,* i.e., isolated or separated by a barrier that keeps out information from other parts of the larger cognitive system, especially from what he calls the "central system." He illustrates this phenomenon with the well-known Müller-Lyer illusion, in which two lines of equal length but differently oriented arrowheads appear to be different in length. In Figure 2.1, the lower line looks longer than the upper one. Fodor points out that the lower line still looks longer even when one knows (e.g., from measurement) that the two lines are really equal in length. This information, though lodged in the central system, does not "penetrate" the visual system or make it produce an equal-length appearance.

Fodor grants that inference is involved in perception. But the scope of information available in perceptual inference, he contends, is sharply delimited. For illustration, he considers the perceptual analysis of speech, in which a parsing mechanism allows people to take acoustic representations of utterances as inputs and produce representations of sentence types (linguistic structural descriptions) as outputs. Since the acoustic character of an utterance underdetermines its structural description, the parser must have access to a lot of background theory. The property of being a noun, for example, has no acoustic correspondent; there's nothing that nouns qua nouns sound like. So a mechanism that can recognize utterances of nouns as such must know something about the language it is parsing, in particular, which words in the language are nouns.

A modular parser for language L, then, might contain a grammar of L that provides information about the linguistic types in L. This information in the grammar would be used inferentially by the parser to produce the perceptual output. But this is *all* of the background information to which the perceptual system can appeal, Fodor suggests. That restriction is what makes it modular.

A New Look parser, by contrast, would be able to bring anything that the organism knows to the process of assigning structural descriptions. Thus, if a hearer knows how very unlikely it is that anyone would say, right smack in the course of a philosophical lecture, "Piglet gave Pooh a stiffening sort of nudge," then, if this utterance actually occurred, the New Look parser would have trouble understanding it precisely because it would be unexpected. Since people obviously would not have trouble understanding this utterance, this suggests to Fodor that the perceptual system is in fact modular.

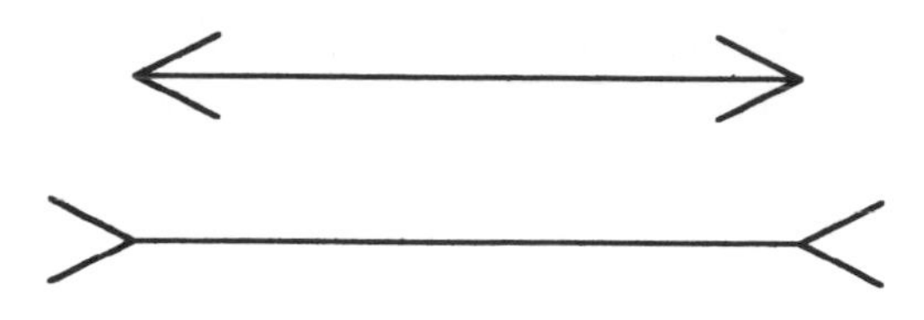

FIGURE 2.1 The Müller-Lyer illusion.

Not having access to the information about the improbability of this utterance's occurrence, the parser is not distracted by such information.

A detailed reply to Fodor has been given by Paul Churchland (1988a), who champions the penetration of perception by theoretical information. Churchland grants that perception often cannot be affected by casual or fleeting attempts to modify the character of one's experience. The Müller-Lyer illusion indeed shows that background information does not easily penetrate visual processing. However, says Churchland, the question is not whether visual processing is *easily* or *quickly* penetrated by contrary information; the issue is whether it is penetrable by long regimes of training, practice, or conditioning. Kuhn claimed that what shapes a scientist's perception is an entire disciplinary matrix that includes standard ways of applying the paradigm, skills acquired during a long apprenticeship. The question, then, is whether perception is "diachronically" penetrable, i.e., penetrable over a long course of experience or learning. Churchland cites research that supports such diachronic penetrability.

Some of this research concerns "inverting lenses," lenses worn over the eyes that invert the orientation of all visual information relative to the body's tactile and motor systems. In short, they turn the visual world upside down. Subjects in inversion experiments gradually manage to recoordinate their vision with the rest of their sensory and motor systems so that the illusion of being in an upside down world fades away in about a week. Thus, information acquired through steady practice and experience, says Churchland, does penetrate our visual processors.

Churchland next argues that even in the case of illusions and visual effects our visual systems are indeed penetrable by higher cognitive assumptions. Ambiguous figures such as the duck/rabbit and the old/young woman are ambiguous with respect to orientation, scale, or perspective. But in all of these cases one learns very quickly to make the figures flip back and forth at will between the two or more alternatives by changing one's assumptions about the nature of the object or the conditions of viewing.

Third, Churchland cites neurophysiological evidence that suggests the systematic penetrability of the peripheral systems by the higher cognitive centers. In the case of vision, the dominant nervous pathway starts at the retina and proceeds via the optic nerve to the lateral geniculate nucleus (LGN) and stepwise from there by other pathways to the primary visual cortex, the secondary visual cortex, and so on. Such "ascending" pathways, however, are almost invariably matched by "descending" pathways. The descending pathways from the visual cortex back to the LGN, for example, are even greater in number than those in the ascending direction. Prima facie, the purpose of these descending pathways is to allow for the modulation of lower level neural activity as a function of the demands sent down from higher levels in the cognitive hierarchy. So the wiring of the brain does not suggest the Fodorian thesis of the encapsulation and isolation of perceptual processing.

Fodor (1988) has in turn replied to Churchland. He grants that the inverted lenses case shows a certain amount of perceptual plasticity. But he regards this as a very special case where some mechanism effects a recalibration between perceptual information and motor movements. This kind of plasticity is obviously needed because an organism's growth requires recalibration of perceived spatial position and bodily gestures. This case does not show, however, that perceptual plasticity is universal, nor does it show that people could somehow reshape their perceptual fields by learning physics.

What about Churchland's claim that one can flip an ambiguous figure, e.g., the duck/rabbit, by "changing one's assumptions"? Fodor denies this. Believing that the figure is a duck doesn't help you see it as one, he says, nor does wanting to see it as a duck help much either. What does produce a flip is changing one's fixation point. In regard to Churchland's neurological data, Fodor claims that no reply is needed. Nobody really knows, at present, what psychological function descending pathways subserve. To say that they subserve the cognitive penetration of perception is sheer speculation.

Whether observation is theory-laden is a debate that will have to be resolved by further empirical research in cognitive science. Of course, philosophical arguments are necessary to assess the implications of the cognitive research. We introduced the problem by presenting a certain philosophical position about the requirements for objectivity in science. This position might be challenged by other philosophical arguments. Granting the plausibility of our earlier philosophical arguments (or arguments to a similar effect), however, it seems clear that research on perception and the perceptual fixation of belief will be crucial to a resolution of the issue.

A Computational Model of Theory Acceptance

Perhaps the central problem in the philosophy of science concerns the evidential conditions in which a scientific theory is (or should be) accepted. Many philosophers of science have sought to characterize these conditions. One approach has been to construct a set of conditions that look rational from the vantage point of deductive logic, inductive logic, and the calculus of probability. Unfortunately, except for deductive logic, these subjects and their application to theory acceptance are highly controversial. Moreover, recent philosophers of science have argued that the older models of scientific rationality often bear little relation to the actual practices of scientists, either in the history of science or in current science. These philosophers and historians demand an empirically accurate account of scientific practice, not just an abstract ideal with minimal connection to concrete scientific research. As W. V. Quine has put it, "Better to discover how science is in fact developed and learned than to fabricate a fictitious structure to a similar effect" (Quine 1969). The task of constructing a descriptively faithful account of scientific reasoning is obviously one that partly falls to cognitive science.

One fruitful way to study such reasoning processes is to build a computational model—a computer program that tries to simulate the reasoning activities in question. By comparing the performance of such a program to actual instances of scientific reasoning, either historical or contemporary, one can judge the descriptive accuracy of the model and then try to improve it. Of course, nobody has direct access to the reasoning procedures of historical scientists against which to compare the program. Written texts by scientists, however, can help identify the hypotheses they accepted, the ones they rejected, and some of their reasons for these decisions. By seeing which hypotheses the program accepts or rejects given the same evidence and background information, one can compare the output of the program to that of historical cases. One attempt to simulate scientific reasoning by means of such a computational model was devised by Paul Thagard (1989). Thagard conjectures that what gives acceptability to a hypothesis is its role in explaining pieces of observed evidence. For example, if a patient is observed to have certain symptoms, and if the presence of disease D would explain or account for those symptoms, then the hypothesis that the patient has disease D becomes somewhat acceptable. Since the explanatory relationship makes the hypothesis "hang together" with the evidence, Thagard speaks of the relationship as one of "coherence." Thus, *explanatory coherence* is the main theme of his approach. Thagard assumes that coherence is a symmetric relation, so that if P coheres with Q, then Q also coheres with P. Similarly, propositions that resist hanging together are said to *incohere*, and if P incoheres with Q, then Q also incoheres with P.

Thagard does not commit himself to any particular theory of explanation. However, he proposes certain plausible-looking principles that link explanation and coherence. His three principles concerning explanation (paraphrased here) are as follows:

> Principle 1: If $P_1 \dots P_m$ jointly explain Q, then each P_i coheres with Q.
> Principle 2: If $P_1 \dots P_m$ jointly explain Q, then each P_i coheres with each P_j.
> Principle 3: In Principles 1 and 2, the degree of coherence is inversely proportional to the number of propositions $P_1 \dots P_m$.

Principle 1 expresses the basic rule that if a hypothesis helps explain something else, then it coheres with it. Principle 2 says that whenever two hypotheses (or "cohypotheses") work together to explain something, these hypotheses cohere with one another. Principle 3 captures the desideratum of explanatory *simplicity*. The fewer the cohypotheses needed to explain proposition Q, the greater the degree of coherence of each explanatory hypothesis with Q and the greater the degree of coherence between the hypotheses themselves.

Now suppose we have a large number of propositions that cohere with one another in accordance with Principles 1, 2, and 3. Does this coherence alone make any one of them worthy of acceptance or belief? Presumably not. We can write a piece of fiction containing a highly coherent set of propositions, but the mere coherence of such a novel does not make it worthy of belief (as descriptive of the actual world). Some members of a coherent system must have a further property that confers believability on them and ultimately on the system as a whole. Thagard calls this the property of *data priority.* He writes this as follows:

> Principle 4: Propositions that describe the results of observation have a degree of acceptability on their own.

In other words, propositions that have been observed to hold true are either fully acceptable (beliefworthy) or at least somewhat acceptable independent of their coherence relations to other propositions. Propositions of this sort are called *evidence,* and pieces of evidence are among the propositions that can be explained by hypotheses. When the propositions are so explained, the degree of coherence between them and their explanatory hypotheses transmits (some degree of) acceptability from them to the hypotheses. These hypotheses can in turn be explained by further (higher-level) hypotheses, and again acceptability is transmitted. Since acceptability is initially transmitted "upwards" from evidence to explanatory hypotheses, a hypothesis that helps to explain many pieces of evidence receives lots of acceptability. This yields a further plausible property of the model, viz., *explanatory breadth.* The more propositions a hypothesis explains (including, directly or indirectly, evidence propositions), the greater its acceptability.

There are two final components in Thagard's scheme. The first of these is *analogy.* Thagard believes that scientists prefer theories that are analogous to theories they already find credible. For example, to the extent that fields of electromagnetic force are analogous to fields of gravitational force, the prior acceptability of the latter made the former more acceptable than they would have been alone. With this in mind he formulates Principle 5:

> Principle 5: If P_1 explains Q_1, P_2 explains Q_2, P_1 is analogous to P_2, and Q_1 is analogous to Q_2, then P_1 and P_2 cohere, and Q_1 and Q_2 cohere.

The final principle in Thagard's scheme (slightly amended here) concerns incoherence:

> Principle 6: If P conflicts with Q, then P and Q incohere.

What is meant here by "conflict" is not just formal inconsistency but also simple incompatibility in light of factual beliefs. Hypotheses viewed as conflicting or competing in a scientific context are often consistent with one another. For example, the hypothesis that a patient has one disease is, strictly speaking, consistent with the hypothesis that he has a second disease (he could have both). But in light of certain background beliefs, the doctor would probably assume that the patient had only one of the two diseases. Thus, the two hypotheses conflict. The crucial role of incoherence is to *reduce* the credibility of hypotheses. If P is highly credible, or acceptable, and P incoheres with Q, then the credibility or acceptability of Q is correspondingly reduced. Given Principle 6, when one hypothesis becomes highly acceptable, it tends to make each rival hypothesis unacceptable in virtue of the relation of incoherence.

Thagard has constructed a computer program called ECHO that embodies the foregoing principles of explanatory coherence. This program applies a certain framework for modeling the mind called *connectionism,* or *parallel distributed processing* (PDP). The underlying idea behind the connectionist framework is to simulate, in a somewhat coarse and approximate fashion, the human brain, viewed as a huge system of connected neurons, each of which engages in interactions with neighboring neurons at the same time as other neurons engage in their interactions. The processing of information does not occur by a series or sequence of single steps but consists in a large number of widely distributed subelements, each of which does its own independent computing. As these distributed units communicate with one another over many rounds or cycles of direct and indirect communication, the system as a whole gradually "settles" into a stable state. This process can sometimes happen very quickly, on the order of seconds or even fractions of a second.

A large number of units are hypothesized in connectionist models. The units can be variously interpreted, but in Thagard's model they represent *propositions* and are assumed to have varying degrees of *activation* ranging between 1 and −1. Positive activation can be interpreted as acceptance of the proposition represented by the unit, negative activation as rejection of the proposition, and activation close to 0 as neutrality. There are two kinds of interunit links: *excitatory* links and *inhibitory* links (patterned after relations found in the brain). If units X and Y are connected via an excitatory link, then activation in unit X raises the activation of unit Y, and vice versa. If units X and Y are connected via an inhibitory link, then activation in unit X lowers the activation of unit Y, and vice versa. Activation can spread through the network of units in a variety of patterns. It is these patterns that have the potential for modeling properties of mental processes, including reasoning processes.

A simple application of the connectionist approach can be illustrated by means of the Necker cube (Figure 2.2). The Necker cube is a reversible figure. By changing the focus of attention, either deliberately or spontaneously, we can easily see it as having either ABCD or EFGH as its frontal face. We are incapable, however, of seeing corner A at the front without also seeing corners B, C, and D at the front. Thus, although more than one visual interpretation of the figure is possible, there are sharp constraints on the feasible interpretations. This process can be modeled in a connectionist network by means of a suitable set of excitatory and inhibitory links between units.

Let Af be a unit that represents the hypothesis that corner A is at the front, while Ab represents the hypothesis that corner A is at the back. Let units Bf, Bb, Cf, Cb, etc., be similarly constructed. To signify that A cannot appear to be both at the front and at the back in any single visual interpretation, we construct an inhibitory link between the units Af and Ab, with similar links inhibiting Bf and Bb, and so on. Because corners A, B, C, and D go together, we construct excitatory links between each pair of Af, Bf, Cf and Df and between each pair of Ab, Bb, Cb, and Db. In addition, we need inhibitory links between Af and Ef, Bf and Ff, and so on. Part of the resulting network is depicted in Figure 2.3, where solid lines indicate excitatory links and dotted lines indicate inhibitory links.

Suppose we focus our attention on corner A, which we assume to be in front, so that unit Af is activated. Then by virtue of the excitatory links from Af to Bf, Cf, and Df, these three units will be activated. The inhibitory links from Af to Ab and Ef will cause those units to be deactivated. In turn, Bb, Cb, and Db will also be deactivated. Thus, activation will spread through the network until all the units corresponding to the view that A, B, C, and D are at the front are activated while all the units corresponding to the view that E, F, G, and H are at the front are deactivated. When the network "settles" into this state, we see face ABCD as being in front and EFGH as being in back. Of course, a few moments later, with a change in focus of attention, the way we see the figure can reverse.

Let us now turn to ECHO, Thagard's connectionist-inspired program for capturing the principles of explanatory coherence. In ECHO, both hypotheses and evidence proposi-

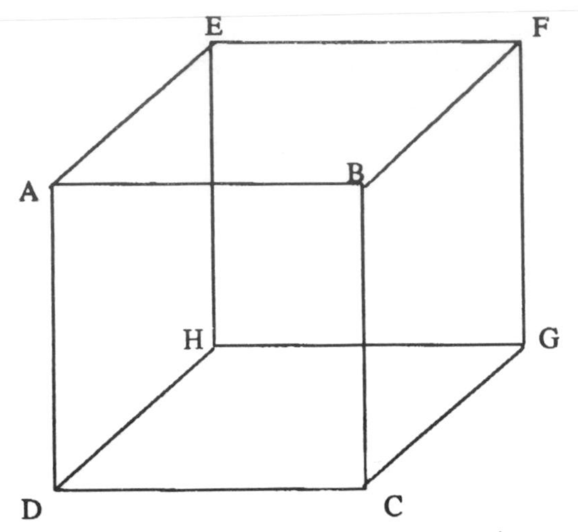

FIGURE 2.2 The Necker cube. Either ABCD or EFGH can be perceived as the front.

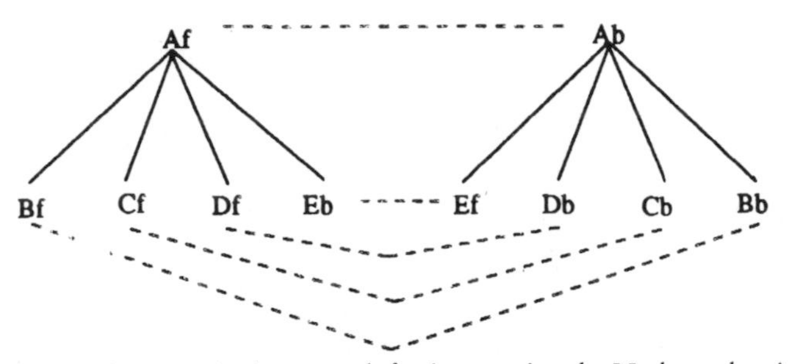

FIGURE 2.3 A connectionist network for interpreting the Necker cube. Af is a unit representing the hypothesis that A is at the front, whereas Ab represents the hypothesis that A is at the back. Solid lines represent excitatory links; dotted lines represent inhibitory links. *Source:* P. Thagard, "Explanatory Coherence," *Behavorial and Brain Sciences* 12 (1989): 435–467. Reprinted by permission of Cambridge University Press.

tions are represented by units. Whenever the principles of explanatory coherence imply that two propositions cohere, an excitatory link between them is established. If two propositions incohere, an inhibitory link is established. Connections between units can also have varying weights. Excitatory links are usually set at .05, and inhibitory weights at around −.20. Since coherence is assumed to be a symmetric relation, the weight from unit 1 to unit 2 is always the same as the weight from unit 2 to unit 1. Since Principle 3 implies that the fewer the cohypotheses required for an explanation, the higher the coherence between the explaining hypotheses and the explained propositions, ECHO attaches higher weights when there are fewer explaining hypotheses.

In accordance with Principle 4 on data priority, each evidence unit receives some activation on its own, quite independently of its connection with other units. When the program is run, activation is first received by evidence units and then spreads to the units representing explanatory hypotheses. Although the data units receive initial activation from outside the system, they are susceptible to deactivation when relations of incoherence result in the decision that a certain "observation" was incorrect.

Runs of the ECHO program show that the connectionist networks using explanatory coherence principles indeed have numerous intuitively desirable properties. Activation accrues to units corresponding to hypotheses that explain more, that provide simpler explanations, and that are analogous to other explanatory hypotheses. The considerations of explanatory breadth, simplicity, and analogy are smoothly integrated. The networks are holistic in the sense that activation of every unit can potentially affect every other unit linked to it, however lengthy the pathway. Nevertheless, the activation of a unit is directly affected only by those units to which it is immediately linked.

Let us look at two very simple networks that could occur in ECHO before turning to a more elaborate example intended to simulate a historical case. First, consider a network with two pieces of evidence, E1 and E2, and two alternative (conflicting) hypotheses, H1 and H2. Suppose H1 explains both E1 and E2, while H2 explains only E2; in other words, H1 has more explanatory breadth than H2. This network is depicted in Figure 2.4. Excitatory links, corresponding to coherence relations, are represented by solid lines, and inhibitory links, corresponding to relations of competition or incoherence, are represented by dotted lines. Since H1 has an explanatory link to both E1 and E2, it receives activation from both of them, whereas H2 receives activation only from E2. Since H1 and H2 are mutually inhibitory, H1 ultimately settles with an activation level above 0, while H2 is deactivated and settles with an activation below 0. Thus, H1 is accepted and H2 rejected.

Now consider a case in which H1 and H2 have the same explanatory breadth, i.e., each explains both E1 and E2, but H1 is itself explained by a further hypothesis, H3, whereas H2 is not explained at all. This scenario is depicted in Figure 2.5. Since being explained by another hypothesis leads to higher coherence, H1 will get more activation than H2. Because H1 and H2 are competitors, and therefore inhibit one another, H1 again settles with activation above 0 (i.e., is accepted), whereas H2 settles with activation below 0 (i.e., is rejected).

Finally, let us see how ECHO can simulate a historical case of scientific reasoning: Charles Darwin's reasoning in favor of his theory of evolution by natural selection. Darwin's two most important hypotheses were:

DH2: Organic beings undergo natural selection.
DH3: Species of organic beings have evolved.

These hypotheses together enabled him to explain a host of facts, from the geographical distribution of similar species to the existence of vestigial organs. Darwin's argument was explicitly comparative, holding that his theory explained phenomena that were inexplicable on the rival, creationist hypothesis that species were separately created by God (CH1), so the factor of explanatory breadth was quite important. Darwin's two main hypotheses were not simply cohy-

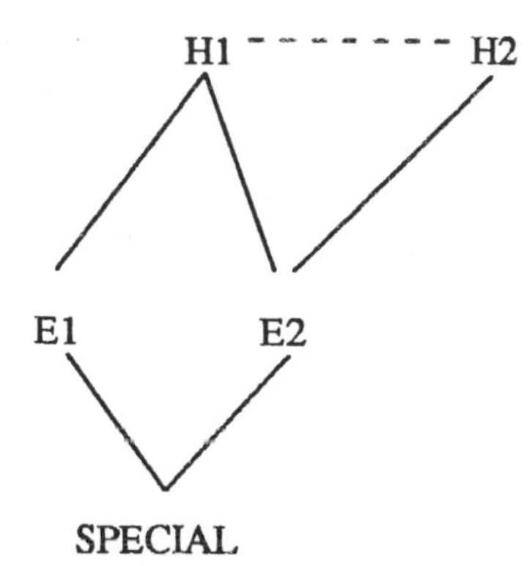

FIGURE 2.4 An ECHO network showing explanatory breadth. As in Figure 2.3, solid lines represent excitatory links, whereas the dotted line represents an inhibitory link. Evidence units E1 and E2 are linked to the special source that activates evidence units. The result of running this network is that H1 defeats H2. *Source:* P. Thagard, "Explanatory Coherence," *Behavioral and Brain Sciences* 12 (1989): 435–467. Reprinted by permission of Cambridge University Press.

potheses, however, for he also used DH2 to explain DH3. Natural selection explained why species evolve: If populations of animals vary, and natural selection picks out for survival those with features well adapted to particular environments, then new species will arise. The full picture also involved the element of analogy. Darwin frequently cited the analogy between artificial selection and natural selection as evidence for his theory. He contended that just as farmers are able to develop new breeds of domesticated animals, so natural selection has produced new species.

The set of hypotheses and evidence propositions in the Darwin case is quite large and complex, and we need not itemize all of them here. But let us enumerate the most relevant ones.

Darwin's main hypotheses
DH1: Organic beings are in a struggle for existence.
DH2: Organic beings undergo natural selection.
DH3: Species of organic beings have evolved.

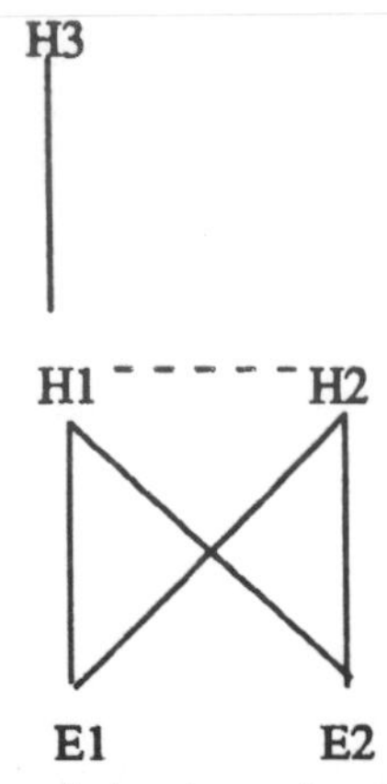

FIGURE 2.5 An ECHO network showing explanation by a higher-level hypothesis. H1 defeats H2 because it is explained by H3. *Source:* P. Thagard, "Explanatory Coherence," *Behavioral and Brain Sciences* 12 (1989): 435–467. Reprinted by permission of Cambridge University Press.

Creationist hypothesis
CH1: Species were separately created by God.

Darwin's evidence
E1: The fossil record contains few transitional forms.
E2: Animals have complex organs.
E3: Animals have instincts.
E4: Species when crossed become sterile.
E5: Species become extinct.
E6: Once extinct, species do not reappear.
E7: Forms of life change almost simultaneously around the world.

Darwin's facts
DF1: Domestic animals undergo variation.
DF2: Breeders select desired features of animals.
DF3: Domestic varieties are developed.

Using these and similar propositions from Darwin's *On the Origin of Species,* Thagard constructs a network featuring explanatory connections (again represented by solid lines), relations of conflict (dotted lines), and relations of analogy (wavy lines). This network is depicted in Figure 2.6. Running ECHO on this network produces the expected result: Darwin's hypotheses are all activated, whereas the creationist hypothesis is deactivated. In particular, the hypothesis DH3—that species evolved—settles at an activation level of .921, while the creationist hypothesis, CH1, declines to −.491.

One might object that in basing ECHO analyses on written texts, one might be modeling the rhetoric or verbalizations of the scientist rather than his mental processes. Presumably, however, there is a close correlation between what the scientist writes and what he or she thinks. In any case, the aim of Thagard's ECHO program is to model the thinking processes of a scientist like Darwin in order to give a descriptively accurate reconstruction of the factors that figured into his theoretical reasoning.

Imagistic Models of Understanding

The traditional view in the philosophy of science emphasized the *logic* of scientific inquiry. Since logic is concerned with relations among propositions or sentences, the received view formulated its models of science in purely propositional or sentential terms. Although this view did not explicitly address the psychology of the scientific thinker, it suggested that scientific thought is exclusively propositional or sentential in character. In the past few years, however, some writers have challenged this depiction of scientific thought from the vantage point of cognitive science, arguing that it neglects the role of visual information and visual imagery in scientific and

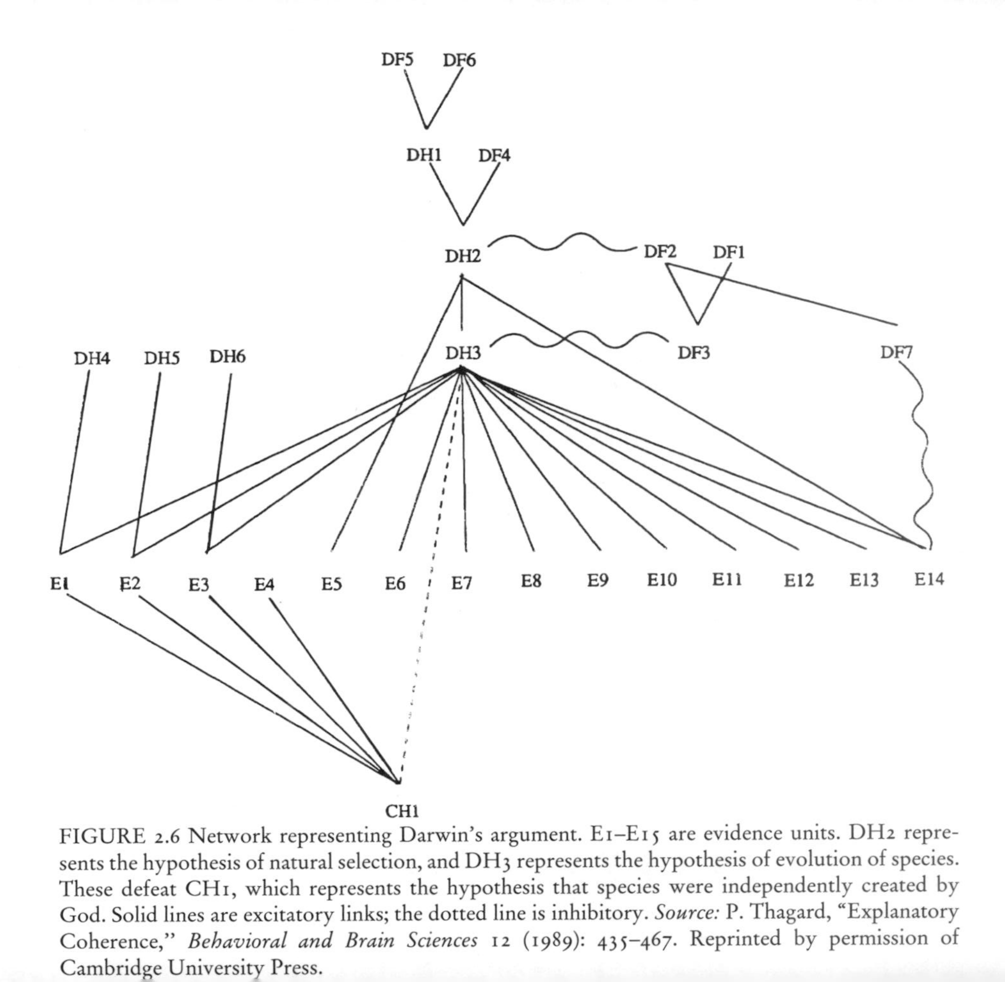

FIGURE 2.6 Network representing Darwin's argument. E1–E15 are evidence units. DH2 represents the hypothesis of natural selection, and DH3 represents the hypothesis of evolution of species. These defeat CH1, which represents the hypothesis that species were independently created by God. Solid lines are excitatory links; the dotted line is inhibitory. *Source:* P. Thagard, "Explanatory Coherence," *Behavioral and Brain Sciences* 12 (1989): 435–467. Reprinted by permission of Cambridge University Press.

mathematical problem solving. (Some theorists maintain that even visual imagery, at bottom, is propositional in form. We shall not enter this area of controversy. In what follows, when we speak of propositional representations, we mean *non-imagistic* propositional representations.)

The significance of visual imagery in human thought has received illuminating treatment in recent cognitive science. Stephen Kosslyn, who has done some of the most important research on visual imagery, describes two significant purposes or functions of imagery (Kosslyn 1990). One purpose is to retrieve information from memory which is not encoded in verbal form. Consider how you would answer the following questions: What shape are a beagle's ears? Which is darker green, a Christmas tree or a frozen pea? Which is bigger, a tennis ball or a 100-watt light bulb? Most people claim that they visualize the objects and "look" at them in order to answer these questions. Thus, we apparently call on some information about object parts and their properties that was previously noticed and stored in memory but not explicitly labeled or categorized at the time. The information is represented in visual form rather than in verbal form. A second purpose of imagery is to anticipate what will happen if physical objects move or are transposed in various ways. For example, we can image a container and "see" whether there is room for it on the top shelf in the refrigerator, or we can mentally project a baseball's trajectory and "see" where it will land. In short, we use imagery to reason about the properties objects will have when they are transformed, relocated, or rearranged.

Roger Shepard and colleagues have extensively studied the second use of imagery and cite anecdotal evidence of its importance in the history of science (Shepard and Cooper 1982). Albert Einstein said explicitly that he very rarely thought in words and that his particular ability did not lie in mathematical calculation but in visualizing effects, consequences, and possibilities. This visualizing, he said, consisted primarily of clear images which he could voluntarily reproduce and combine. James Watson's account of how he and Francis Crick deciphered the double-helical structure of DNA contains still more specific references to the mental performance of spatial transformations. Watson had the sudden, crucial realization that under an appropriate rotation in space an adenine-thymine pair was identical in shape to a guanine-cytosine pair, and when he then went into the laboratory, he found Crick flipping cardboard base pairs about an imaginary line.

The widespread use of diagrams in scientific and mathematical problem solving is further evidence of the convenience and power of visualization as a cognitive instrument. Jon Barwise and John Etchemendy illustrate this notion with the help of the following puzzle.

> You are to seat four people, A, B, C, and D, in a row of five chairs. A and C are to flank the empty chair. C must be closer to the center than D, who is to sit next to B. From this information, show that the empty chair is not in the middle or on either end. Can you tell who must be seated in the center? Can you tell who is to be seated on the two ends? (Barwise and Etchemendy 1991, 14)

People who solve this problem typically employ reasoning that features a large visual component; they may find it useful to draw some diagrams. For example, one may start with the following diagram to represent the five chairs.

— — — — —

Our first piece of information tells us that A and C are to flank the empty chair. Let us use x to signify that a chair is empty. Then we can consider six possible cases. Or, since the problem does not distinguish left from right, we can limit our attention to three cases (the others being mirror images of them).

Case 1	Case 2	Case 3
A X C _ _	_ A X C _	_ _ A X C

Using the fact that C must be seated closer to the center than D, we can eliminate Case 3, since C is not closer than any available chair. Similarly, since D must sit next to B, we can rule out Case 2, since no contiguous chairs are available. This leaves us with two possibilities:

Case 1.1	Case 1.2
A X C B D	A X C D B

All of the stated constraints are satisfied in both cases, and so we know that neither case can be ruled out. This allows us to answer the question posed in the puzzle. First, in both cases the empty chair is not in the middle or on either end, as desired. Second, C must be seated in the middle. Finally, A must be on one end of the row, but we do not know whether B or D is on the other end.

It is evident from this illustration how helpful diagrams can be. Organizing the possibilities in a visual format makes it easier, intuitively, to keep track of them and detect their relevant properties. Barwise and Etchemendy claim that such forms of visual representation can be essential and can legitimate components in valid deductive reasoning. They do not doubt that a solution to the foregoing problem could be worked out with a standard system of deduction using a purely propositional or sentential format. They do claim, however, that such a system would be vastly more complex than the solution using diagrams (or visualizations of such diagrams). They further suggest that visualization of this sort plays a much bigger role in mathematical proofs than is generally acknowledged and that this partly accounts for the discrepancy between actual mathematical proofs and their formal idealizations. In calculus, for example, the concept of a continuous function is linguistically expressed with the help of the usual $\epsilon - \delta$ terminology; nonetheless, the basic ideas are essentially visual ones. That is why, when giving proofs, mathematicians often shortcut the $\epsilon - \delta$ characterization and rely more directly on the visual concept. Barwise and Etchemendy also note that people seem to have difficulty in mastering the art of formal (i.e., sentential) proof construction. If visualization plays a bigger role in mathematical proof than has generally been recognized, the difficulty may be due to the fact that purely formal proofs are foreign to their style of cognitive representation.

Is Numerical Knowledge Innate?

As we noted in Chapter 1, philosophers have long disputed the role of inborn factors in the acquisition of knowledge. On the topic of mathematics, rationalists like Immanuel Kant (1787/1965) maintained that mathematical truths are a product of our native faculties and hence are knowable a priori. Empiricists like John Stuart Mill (1843/1881) contended that mathematical truths can only be known a posteriori, that is, through perceptual experience. Mill held that we learn truths about numbers, such as that one plus two equals three, by observing it to be true for sheep in one instance, for cookies in another instance, and so on, until we finally induce that it is true in all cases.

Among contemporary philosophers, Philip Kitcher (1983, 1988) has spelled out an empiricist view of numerical knowledge in the most detail. He suggests that individuals learn simple mathematical facts from observing the results of their own actions and learn the rest of mathematics from parents, teachers, and other authorities, who in turn get their knowledge from mathematics experts. A fundamental numerical fact, like one plus two equals three, is learned by "collecting" one item, collecting two different items, combining these collections, and observing that the result is equivalent to the action of collecting three items. So basic truths of arithmetic are learned through such activities as collecting and segregating.

Approaching this proposal in cognitive terms, Karen Wynn (1992b) asks for a more precise account of the kinds of actions and observations that are supposed to be critical for knowledge of numerical truths. If the actions of collecting and segregating must be overtly performed on physical objects by each individual knower, this theory would predict that quadriplegics, for example, could not arrive at these numerical truths. If the relevant actions need only be mental actions, we could no longer sustain an empiricist theory, since the relevant knowledge could be acquired independent of perceptual experience. Wynn also points to substantial experimental evidence that knowledge of basic numerical concepts and relations is not learned. Let us survey this research (as summarized by Wynn) in support of a nativist approach to numerical knowledge.

Studies have shown that five-month-olds (Starkey and Cooper 1980) and even newborns (Antell and Keating 1983) are able to discriminate small numerosities. They can tell two from three, and under certain conditions, three from four. These studies used a habituation technique in which infants are repeatedly presented with ("habituated to") different pictures showing a certain number of objects until the amount of time they spend looking at each picture drops below a designated criterion. They are then shown a picture either of that same number of objects again or of a different number of objects. Infants tend to look significantly longer at (to "dishabituate to") the picture depicting a new number of objects than at the picture depicting the same number, indicating that they can differentiate between the two numerosities. Furthermore, the knowledge underlying this ability is not local to visual perception. Infants can recognize numerical equivalence across perceptual modalities. When six- to nine-month-old infants heard tape recordings of either two knocks or three knocks, then shown simultaneously a picture of two items and a picture of three items, they preferred to look at the picture showing the number of items corresponding to the number of knocks heard (Starkey, Spelke, and Gelman, 1983, 1990). Thus, the basis for infants' abilities to recognize differences and equivalences between instances of small numbers seems to be an abstract and conceptual representation of number, not just some kind of perceptual pattern-recognition.

Other animals are also sensitive to exact numerosities, as many studies have shown. For example, rats are able to determine the number of times they have pressed on a lever, up to at least twenty-four presses, when trained to press a certain number of times on a particular lever before pressing a single time on a second lever for a reward. Rats have also been trained (Davis and Bradford 1986) to turn down the third, fourth, or fifth tunnel on the left in a maze, and once trained, they will continue to do so even when the spatial configuration of the maze is varied from trial to trial so that the distance between the tunnels changes, and a corner must be turned before the rewarded tunnel is reached. Thus, the rats could not just be running for a fixed length of time before turning left. They must be encoding the number of tunnels passed on the left in order to succeed.

Birds have shown similar abilities. Pastore (1961) trained canaries to select an object based on its ordinal position in an array. Out of ten cubicles spaced along a runway, the canaries had to choose the cubicle that held, say, the fifth aspirin. Both the space between cubicles and the number of aspirins per cubicle were varied so that the birds' success depended on encoding the ordinal position of the aspirin.

It may be objected that neither infants nor animals are likely to grasp an *abstracted* concept of twoness, as opposed to recognizing a pair of pheasants or a pair of boots. But studies have shown that infants recognize the common attribute of twoness across different kinds of items, and animals will generalize a response to new kinds of items.

Not only are animals and infants sensitive to numerosity, but they can also perform basic arithmetical calculations over these numerosities. The most conclusive evidence of an animal's ability to perform addition is shown in the following experiment. Boysen and Berntson (1989) taught a chimpanzee to associate the Arabic numerals "0" through "4" with their respective numerosities. Without further training, she was able to choose the numeral representing the sum of oranges hidden in two hiding places. Most impressive of all, when the sets of oranges in the hiding places were replaced with Arabic numerals, she was immediately able to choose the Arabic numeral representing the sum of these numerals.

These results show that upon computing the numerosity of some set of items or events, animals can compare the symbol for this numerosity with others stored in memory and compute some precise arithmetical relationships. Similarly, Wynn (1992a) has found that human infants as young as five months appear to be able to calculate the precise outcome of simple additions and subtractions. Infants were divided into two groups. Those in the "1 + 1" group first saw two identical items being successively placed into a display area. Because of a hiding procedure, however, they could not see the result of this arithmetical operation. Infants in the "2 − 1" group were similarly presented with a sequence of events depicting a subtraction of one item from two items. After these sequences were concluded, the hidden object(s) were revealed and the infants' looking time was recorded. Wynn's prediction was that infants in the "1 + 1" group should look longer when the result was 1 (an apparently impossible result if the correct sum was computed) than when it was 2, while infants in the "2 − 1" group should show the reverse pattern. This was in fact the pattern of the results obtained.

Since these results seem to suggest innate capacities to represent numbers and compute numerical relationships, what might be a mechanism that would explain these capacities? Meck and Church (1983) propose the *accumulator* theory, which hypothesizes a single mechanism to explain animals' abilities to determine numerosity and measure duration. This mechanism includes a pacemaker that puts out pulses at a constant rate, which can then pass into an accumulator by the closing of a mode switch. Every time an entity to be counted passes through, the mode switch closes for a fixed interval, passing energy into the accumulator. Thus, the accumulator fills up in equal increments, one for each entity counted. The final value in the accumulator passes into working memory and is compared with previously stored accumulator values. Thus, the animal can evaluate whether a number of events is more, less, or the same as a previously stored number associated with some outcome, such as a reward. Wynn suggests that such a mechanism could underlie infants' performances as well as those of animals.

Another nativist theory of numerical knowledge has been proposed by Rochel Gelman and colleagues (Gelman and Gallistel 1978; Gelman and Greeno 1989). They propose that young children possess an innate concept of number consisting of a set of counting principles to define correct counting and a set of mental counting tags that are used in accordance with these principles. The three "how-to-count" principles are as follows: (1) the *one-to-one correspondence* principle, which states that items to be counted must be put into one-to-one correspondence with members of the set of number tags that are used to count with; (2) the *stable-order* principle, which states that the number tags must have a fixed order in which they are consistently used; and (3) the *cardinality* principle, which states that the last number tag used in a count represents the cardinality of the items counted.

These principles are thought to provide an initial skeletal framework that shapes and structures the child's developing body of numerical knowledge. The principles make it easier for children to learn the number words of their language and to map them onto their own innately given list of number tags, which operate in accordance with the same principles as number words. Thus, the counting principles help children to identify early on the linguistic, culturally supported counting activity as *counting*, i.e., as the same kind of activity as their own innate, nonlinguistic counting activity.

The widespread evidence supporting a nativist approach to numerical knowledge (in a loose sense of "knowledge"), in conjunction with the two possible models of how that knowledge might be realized, provide an intriguing example of how cognitive science can reveal the mental underpinnings of mathematical (and hence scientific) knowledge. Speculation about the nature of mathematical understanding, which goes back as far as Plato's *Meno*, may ultimately be settled by empirical research in cognitive science.

Suggestions for Further Reading

The Fodor-Churchland debate on the theory-ladenness of perception appears in Fodor (1984) [R], Fodor (1988), and P. M. Churchland (1988a) [R]. The background on Fodor's modularity approach is in Fodor (1983); the ubiquity of theory is defended in Churchland (1979).

Thagard (1989) [R] explains the program ECHO and its applications. Thagard (1992) extends these ideas to conceptual and revolutionary change in science. A somewhat different artificial intelligence approach to scientific inquiry is presented by Langley, Simon, Bradshaw, and Zytkow (1987) [R]. Other works that seek cognitivistic descriptions of scientific activity include Holland, Holyoak, Nisbett, and Thagard (1986), Churchland (1989), and Giere (1988).

Carey (1985) and Keil (1989) draw on theories of conceptual change in science to model conceptual change in children.

The nature and role of imagery are addressed by Kosslyn (1980, 1990). Theoretical debates about imagery are featured in Block (1981), Pinker (1985), and Tye (1991).

Wynn (1992b) [R] explores the evidence for an innate knowledge of number.

Chapter Three

Philosophy of Mind

This chapter takes a slightly different approach to its subject than the others. About two thirds of the chapter is "pure" philosophy of mind, which does not draw from the literature in cognitive science. It is related to cognitive science, however, for two reasons. First, recent approaches to the philosophy of mind develop perspectives on the mind that are highly congenial to the "functional" and "computational" models that are so popular in cognitive science. Second, issues in the philosophy of mind are often closely intertwined with choices of research strategies in cognitive science. The final third of the chapter, moreover, transforms questions in philosophy of mind into questions for cognitive science. How people ordinarily represent or understand mental concepts (a central problem in philosophy of mind) is ultimately an empirical problem requiring theoretical and experimental investigations appropriate to cognitive science.

Dualism and Materialism

The metaphysical nature of the mind is one of the main problems of philosophy. It took center stage in the early modern period when Descartes argued that the mind is something wholly nonphysical and nonmaterial. Descartes offered several reasons for this view. First, he claimed that he could know of his own existence as a purely thinking entity without supposing that he had a body or a brain at all. From this he concluded that he must have a nature or essence that is not dependent on anything bodily or physical. Second, he claimed that the mind is whole and indivisible, whereas anything physical or material is composed of parts and is therefore divisible. Third, Descartes did not believe that anything physical is capable of mathematical reasoning, the mastery of language, or consciousness. Thus, Descartes claimed that there are two basically different kinds of entities or substances: (1) physical entities, which fill space and have size and weight, and (2) minds, which have no physical characteristics whatever. Descartes agreed that there is a regular causal interaction between minds and physical things. Each human being is a complex entity consisting of a mind specially connected with a particular body (including the brain). But these two components, the mind and the body, are totally different in nature. This view is called mind-body *dualism.*

At least two worries about dualism immediately arise. First, Descartes' immaterial minds are rather queer, ghostly entities; they have no mass, shape, or position anywhere in space. Their only properties are those associated with thinking, feeling, or perceiving. Second, it is very difficult to understand how an entity of this sort could causally interact with something physical. Yet Descartes himself posited causal interaction, and such interaction seems inescapable. When my finger is accidentally smashed, my mind feels pain; when my ears are in close proximity to the ocean, my mind hears the soothing sounds of the sea; and when my mind resolves to dive into the ocean, here and now, my body jumps right in. Thus, the body causally affects the mind, and the mind causally affects the body. But how can this happen if the mind does not fill space and has no mechanical, chemical, electrical, or other physical properties? How can the body exert any force on, or effect any change in, the mind? And how can the nonspatial, nonphysical mind effect any change in the body?

The Identity Theory

These worries have induced many thinkers to reject mind-body dualism. The most popular alternative, *materialism*, claims that there is only one kind of reality in the world: physical (or material) reality. (Physical reality, in this context, includes such things as energy, fields of force, and so on.) Contemporary materialists typically agree that there are minds but deny that they are the sorts of substances Descartes claimed them to be. Instead, they are just highly complex forms of matter, such as brains or central nervous systems. A mind, in other words, is not something above and beyond or separate from the brain; it is one and the same thing as a brain. This form of materialism, called the *identity theory*, easily solves the puzzle of mind-body interaction. Since the mind is itself something physical, there is no mystery about how it can causally interact with the rest of the body.

One question about the identity theory is: How do we decide which physical thing the mind is to be identified with? Why say it is identical with the brain or the central nervous system rather than the heart or the entire body? The answer here depends on information from various branches of science including, of course, the neurosciences. These sciences tell us that all known mental phenomena are specially dependent on parts of the brain or aspects of neural activity but may be relatively independent of what happens in other bodily organs. Rational thought is affected when alcohol or narcotics reach certain portions of the brain or when there is senile degeneration of nerve tissue. Anesthetics or caffeine, when appropriately introduced into the brain, have marked effects on consciousness, and particular regions of the brain are known to be directly associated with specific mental faculties, such as vision or language.

Does it make sense to identify the mind with anything physical? This identification may sound strange. When you focus attention inward, on your mind and its contents, what you find are thoughts, sensations, and emotions. You don't find a neural network exhibiting electrochemical activity. How could two things be more different than the mind and the brain?

The reply of the identity theorist is that we may apprehend one and the same object through different modes of acquaintance that reveal different aspects or properties of the object. The two modes of acquaintance make it appear as if two distinct objects are the targets of our apprehension, whereas in fact there is just one thing. Imagine, for instance, two separate sightings of a certain peak, one from the east and one from the west. The peak may appear quite different from these two perspectives, and a mountaineer might not recognize it as the very same peak. Nonetheless, it is one and the same. Similarly, the kind of acquaintance that a neurosurgeon has with a patient's brain is entirely different from that patient's own acquaintance with his brain. The patient "experiences" his brain by undergoing its processes and changes of state; he has a distinctive mode of internal access to his brain called *introspection.* The neurosurgeon, on the other hand, can only see or touch the brain. It is not surprising that these forms of access generate distinct types of appearances.

Dualists have sometimes responded to identity theorists by saying that we *mean* or *understand* something entirely different by the terms "mind" and "brain"; we *conceptualize* these entities quite differently. So how is it possible that the two should really be one and the same? Identity theorists have a ready response to this objection. It is perfectly possible, they say, that two distinct conceptualizations should nonetheless denote one and the same entity. You may conceptualize your town mayor quite differently from the way you conceptualize the person who picked your pocket in the crowd last night. You may think of the former as an upstanding businessman, the latter as a nefarious sneak. Nonetheless, it could turn out that these individuals are one and the same! Analogously, although our concept of "mind" is quite different from our concept of "brain," the referents or *designata* of these terms could turn out to be one and the same thing.

A generally accepted requirement for identity is this: If object x is identical to object y, then any property of x must also be a property of y (and vice versa). This principle is called *the indiscernibility of identicals.* If Superman is a heroic man of steel who flies faster than a speeding bullet and sports a flashy blue and red outfit, and if Clark Kent is identical to Superman, then Clark Kent must also be a heroic man of steel who flies faster than a speeding bullet and sports a flashy blue and red outfit. In fact, Superman and Clark Kent do possess exactly the same properties.

What about the mind and the brain? The identity theorist claims that all properties possessed by the mind are possessed by the brain and vice versa. Just as the mind is the "seat" of thinking and feeling, so the brain is the seat of thinking and feeling. Just as the brain undergoes electrochemical processes, so the mind undergoes electrochemical processes. In some cases, our prescientific conceptualization of the mind may be mistaken. Descartes, says the identity theorist, was wrong when he said that the mind was indivisible. As far as physical capacities for mathematical reasoning, language learning, and consciousness are concerned, Descartes was again mistaken. Certain physical things, including at least the brain, do have these capacities. Hence, the identity theorist concludes, nothing stands in the way of the identification of mind and brain.

Property Dualism

The dualist is not yet ready to throw in the towel. He typically grants, at this juncture, that minds are not a distinct kind of nonphysical *substance.* He still suspects, though, that mental *properties* comprise a special class of nonphysical properties, even if they are properties possessed by a physical substance. Each mental property, such as having pain, having a sensation of red, being intelligent, or believing proposition P, is entirely distinct from any physical property. Thus, having abandoned *substance dualism,* he still clings to *property dualism.*

The property dualist characteristically retains much of Descartes' conception of mental properties. To be in pain is to have a particular sort of private, conscious, introspective feeling. No physical property is the same as this. There might well be some physical property that is *correlated* with being in pain. Perhaps there is a certain class of neural fibers, call them "C-fibers," such that a person is in pain when and only when his C-fibers fire. Nonetheless, says the property dualist, C-fiber firing isn't *the same thing as* (isn't the same property as) being in pain.

There is a variant of the identity theory which claims not only that each mental property has a correlated neural property (such as C-fiber firing) but that such pairs of correlated properties are really *identical.* In this view, the property of being in pain *is* the property of having one's C-fibers fire, and having the property of seeing red *is* the property of (say) having certain cells activated in the visual cortex. This doctrine is called *type-type* identity theory (or type-type materialism). The property dualist, by contrast, denies that such pairs of correlated properties are identical or even that a uniquely correlated neural property must exist for each mental property.

To many philosophers, the prospect of property dualism is just as disconcerting as substance dualism. It seems to bifurcate nature in a mysterious way. For these philosophers, the metaphysics of property dualism ruins an otherwise streamlined uniformity throughout nature. This is one reason they seek to avoid property dualism and secure a thoroughgoing materialism.

Philosophical Behaviorism

Philosophical behaviorism offers a theory of mental properties focusing on the *meanings* of the words by which such properties are expressed. Words and expressions such as "pain," "perception of red," "intelligent," and "belief" are not to be understood as referring to ghostly inner episodes but as referring to overt, publicly observable behavior or dispositions to behave in certain ways. If this is all we *mean* by such language, then this language does not introduce any nonphysical properties. Thus, behaviorism promises a very thoroughgoing materialism that avoids both property dualism and substance dualism.

Behaviorism came into fashion in the 1940s and 1950s with the help of certain background doctrines. First, there was the *verificationist* doctrine of meaning, which held that the meaning of any sentence resides in the observable events or circumstances that verify or confirm its truth. Verificationism was thought to embody the proper methodology of science because its assertions could be checked or verified in an intersubjective or public arena. Thus, the scientific meaning of a sentence would be restricted to the empirical or experimental outcomes that could be derived or predicted from the sentence. Behaviorism applied this idea further and held that the meaning of a sentence ascribing a mental property consists in a special kind of behavior or behavioral tendency implied by that sentence.

A second background argument was the *private-language* argument advanced by Ludwig Wittgenstein (1953). Wittgenstein attempted to show that what he called a necessarily private language, a language referring to objects or events that are necessarily private in the sense that nobody else could have any access to them, is impossible. Suppose you attempt to give meaning to the term "W" by associating it with some purely private sensation. At a later time, upon feeling a sensation, you may say: "There is another W." How can you tell, though, whether you are using the term correctly on this occasion? Are you following the meaning rule you fixed for "W" originally? Perhaps you misremember the first sensation and thereby misremember the rule you gave yourself. Since there is no way to distinguish a correct use and an incorrect use of "W" (and nobody else can help you since, by hypothesis, nobody else has access to the events in question), the term really does not have any meaning. The only meaning rules that are legitimate are those that invoke public objects and events. Words stand in need of an "outer" criterion of application, not a purely "inner" criterion.

By means of these arguments (whatever their real cogency), philosophical behaviorists became convinced that mental terms should be given behavioral definitions that would parallel dispositional definitions for certain nonmental terms. To say that a sugar cube is "soluble," for example, is to say that if it were immersed in water, it would dissolve. In other words, the sugar has a *disposition to behave* in a certain way if placed in certain circumstances. Analogously, to say that someone is angry is to say that he is disposed to frown or scowl or to fly into a rage if provoked. To say that someone has a pain in his leg is to say that he will tend to limp on that leg, or favor it, or wince if you touch it in the painful spot.

Obviously, an accurate behavioral definition of a mental term will have to be rather complex. This much was always conceded. To illustrate, let us look at a behaviorist-style definition of the term "intelligence" proposed by Alan Turing, who was instrumental in laying the theoretical foundations for the modern computer. Turing (1950) proposed that whether a machine is intelligent depends on whether it can pass the following "behavioral" test. A judge is placed in one room and allowed to communicate by teletype (this was 1950) with a computer in a second room and a person in a third room. The judge is supposed to figure out which party is the computer and which is the person. The computer tries to fool the judge into thinking that it is the person, so it tries to imitate a person. The machine is intelligent, according to Turing, if it can win at this "imitation game." This test of intelligence is behavioristic in the sense that it doesn't require that the machine have any conscious thoughts or other specific "inner" episodes in order to qualify as intelligent. It just has to *behave* in a way that will fool the judge (or make the judge's guess no better than chance).

Is behaviorism correct? Can mental predicates be defined in purely behavioral terms? Here are several objections commonly lodged against behaviorism. First, by making the criteria of mental properties purely "outer," behaviorism misses what seems crucial to our understanding of these properties: the "inner" aspect. It seems as if an anesthetized person would count as being in pain if he had the right behavioral dispositions—and that seems plainly wrong. Second, the connection between mental states and behavior is not as tight as the behaviorist alleges. Is it necessarily true that a person in pain is prone to cry or wince or evince some other "sign" or "manifestation" of his pain? Apparently not. Borrowing an example from Hilary Putnam (1963), consider a person raised in a highly Spartan culture that trains children to suppress any and all expressions of pain or discomfort. Such a person can be in pain without behaving in any of the standard pain-related ways. A third problem is that it is impossible to give a correct definition of many mental terms without introducing other mental terms into the definition. Consider the mental predicate "believes that it's raining outside." A promising behavioral definition might be: "If X went outside, X would take an umbrella." On reflection, though, this definition is wrong. Someone who believes it is raining would take an umbrella if he dislikes getting wet, but not if he enjoys getting wet. Accordingly, the definition might be amended as follows: "If X went outside and wanted to avoid getting wet, X would take an umbrella." The trouble with the revised definition is that it doesn't define the belief predicate in purely behavioral terms. The defining expression uses the term "want, " which is itself a mental predicate. This kind of problem turns out to be endemic. No belief predicate can be given a correct dispositional definition without invoking desire predicates; no desire predicate can be defined without invoking belief predicates; and so on for many other mental predicates. Clearly, the states that mental predicates denote interact in systematic ways with states denoted by other mental predicates, and this interaction is important to their meaning.

Functionalism

Functionalism, an heir of behaviorism, also tries to account for the meanings of mental expressions ultimately in terms of external events (stimuli and behavior) without succumbing to behaviorism's pitfalls. Unlike behaviorism, functionalism acknowledges that mental states are "inner" states. But it is not the *intrinsic* quality of an inner state that makes a mental state what it is. Rather, it is the state's *causal relations:* first, its relations to external events such as stimulus inputs and behavioral outputs and second, its relations to other internal states. Thus, functionalism does not ignore the interaction among internal states.

An example from David Lewis (1966), one of the originators of functionalism, illustrates a basic functional definition. What does it mean for a regular combination lock to be "unlocked"? It means that the lock is in some internal state S such that (1) S is caused by setting the lock (turning the right combination), and (2) S causes the lock to open when gently pulled. Notice that the definition says nothing about the intrinsic character of the state of "unlockedness." It explains unlockedness purely in terms of its relations to "external" events (actual or possible). Functional definitions typically include a specification of how the target state (causally) relates to other internal states as well. However, those other internal states themselves receive no intrinsic description in a functional definition. They too are only defined, ultimately, in terms of relations to external events. Thus, functional definitions simultaneously introduce a number of internal-state concepts which are jointly explained in terms of their (causal) relations to external events and to one another.

How does this method work in the case of mental predicates? The functionalist claims that in learning the meaning of mental predicates, people learn causal laws of three types: (A) laws relating environmental events and mental states, (B) laws relating mental states and other mental states, and (C) laws relating mental states and overt behavior. Here are some examples.

(A_1) If a part of the body is cut or damaged or burned, then the person will be in pain.
(A_2) If a red tomato is directly in front of a person in ample light, then the person will have a perception of red.
(A_3) If a person has gone many hours without liquid, he will tend to be thirsty.
(B_1) If a person is thirsty, he will tend to want to drink.
(B_2) If a person wants to drink, and if he believes that a potable liquid is in the refrigerator, he will form an intention to go to the refrigerator.
(B_3) If a person believes proposition P, and if he believes "if P then Q," then he will tend to believe Q.

(C_1) If a person is in severe pain, he will tend to wince and/or groan.
(C_2) For any actions X and Y, if a person decides to do X and believes that Y is the best way to do X (and he is able to do Y), then he will do Y.
(C_3) If a person is happy, he will tend to smile.

Let "I" stand for environmental input, "S" for internal state, and "O" for behavioral output. Then the first three generalizations are I-S generalizations, the second three are S-S generalizations, and the final three are S-O generalizations.

Given such generalizations, the functionalist claims that each mental expression can be understood only in terms of its relations to inputs, other internal states, and outputs. This understanding of mental expressions does not appeal to "intrinsic" qualities—what pain or thirst or belief "feels like"—but only to these relations.

Like behaviorism, functionalism is congenial to materialism because it defines mental predicates ultimately in terms of their relations to physical inputs and outputs. Functionalism must also be distinguished, however, from type-type materialism. Indeed, the originator of one brand of functionalism, Hilary Putnam, offered an argument against type-type materialism as a reason in favor of functionalism (Putnam 1967). Putnam pointed out that it is extremely unlikely that a given mental property, such as pain, has the same neural form in all organisms. An octopus surely feels pain, but since its mollusk brain is rather different from the human or mammalian brain, its pains are probably not correlated with the same neural states as ours. In the absence of a systematic neural correlation, pain (in general) cannot be identified with, or realized in, any particular neural state. This argument is called the argument from *multiple realizability.* The proper status of pain, then, is purely functional. What is constitutive of pain is not an underlying neural character but its *functional role,* that is, its distinctive combination of relations to environmental inputs, other internal states, and behavioral outputs. Functionalists often compare pain and other mental states to functionally defined entities like a valve lifter or a mousetrap (see Fodor 1968). What makes an engine part a valve lifter is that, given a specified input, it has a certain output, namely, the lifting of the valves. Such a device might be instantiated in a variety of physical ways. Similarly, a mousetrap is a functional kind of object that might be implemented in all manner of physically different devices: spring traps, cage traps, and so forth.

Cognitive Science and the Functional "Level"

The functionalist conception of mental states is often regarded as highly congenial to cognitive science because it provides a model that is both "inner" and yet amenable to scientific investigation. It specifies a level of analysis above the neural or physiological and therefore congenial to cognitive psychology and artificial intelligence. Hard-core functionalists contend that the cognitive organization of an organism should be studied in terms of input-output relations or information-flow patterns rather than in terms of the material or structural realizations of the cognitive events in question. The cognitive scientist, says the functionalist, is interested in the psychological processes or algorithms used by the mind. One and the same psychological algorithm or program can be subserved by alternate structural implementations, just as a program written in BASIC can be executed by two computers with different hardware and different assembly languages. According to functionalism, cognitive science can abstract from the hardware level and focus on the program level. Thus, functionalists draw an analogy between mental states and programs, because both are characterized at a functional level rather than a structural or implementational level. Indeed, it has been popular to describe the mind as "the program run by the brain."

This hard-core version of functionalism has its vocal critics. Patricia Churchland (1986), for example, argues that it invites too sharp a separation between cognitive science and neuroscience. Instead of an isolationist or "top-down" strategy of functionalism, she endorses a "coevolutionary" research program that assigns equally important roles to the functional and structural (or neural) levels.

Computationalism and the Language of Thought

Philosophers of mind usually divide mental states into two categories: (1) sensations, like pains, itches, and perceptual appearances, and (2) propositional attitudes, such as thinking, believing, wanting, and intending. The critical feature of attitudes is their "content" or "aboutness": They typically refer to objects in the world, which they "represent" as being one way or another. Thus, they have a representational or semantical character, often called "intentionality." One crucial question in the philosophy of mind is how thoughts and other mental states get their intentional or representational character.

One partial (but only partial!) answer to this question is that thoughts have content by virtue of having a structure analogous to sentences of English or other natural languages. Jerry Fodor, in particular, has argued that mental representation requires a medium of representation—that some sort of language is required no less in the human mind than in computers (Fodor 1975, 1980, 1987). Computers employ machine languages of various kinds, and it is plausible to postulate that a human "machine language" is the vehicle of human thought and cognition. Fodor calls this "the language of thought"

(LOT), or sometimes "mentalese." Fodor claims that every propositional attitude is a relation between a person (the bearer of that attitude) and a sentence in LOT. "Believing" is one such relation, "intending" another relation, and so forth. Or, according to a popular metaphor, "believing" is a matter of having sentences of mentalese stored in the "belief box." What distinguishes one belief from another is the particular sentence of mentalese that appears in the belief box. Mental processes, such as making a deductive inference or changing one's plans, are computational operations using symbols in LOT.

Several objections have been lodged against the LOT hypothesis. One of these, registered both by Daniel Dennett (1986) and Patricia Churchland (1980, 1986), is that a sentence-crunching picture of the brain seems profoundly unbiological. Churchland poses an evolutionary dilemma for the defender of LOT. Either sentence processing arises early in phylogeny, or the sentence processing of human cognizers has no precedent in the mental processes of other organisms. The first alternative seems wildly implausible to Churchland; it seems highly unlikely that nonlinguistic or prelinguistic organisms possess a complete LOT. (She calls this the "infralinguistic catastrophe.") The second alternative is unsatisfactory because members of nonlinguistic species seem perfectly capable of cognition, e.g., rational planning. So there should be evolutionary continuity, not a sharp break between infrahumans and humans.

The issue over the existence of LOT is part of the philosophy of mind, but also poses a question about the "best bet" for successful model-building in cognitive science. Should cognitive science pursue its study of the mind with the help of the LOT hypothesis? Or will cognitive science find more fruitful theoretical constructs by rejecting this notion? The putative value of the LOT approach has been sharply challenged by the advent of connectionist models of cognition that provide an alternative to the classical "rules and representations" approach.

As indicated in Chapter 2, a connectionist architecture consists of simple units, each of which has a determinate degree of activation at any time and is connected to a number of other units to which it sends inhibitory or excitatory stimuli. When given an initial pattern of activation, the excitations and inhibitions passing through the system will alter the activation states of the units until a stable pattern is achieved. A connectionist system is massively parallel—in other words, the various units in the system all compute at the same time—and its operation constitutes a kind of continuous dynamical system. According to one leading view (Smolensky 1988), the numerical variables in the system correspond to fine-grained features below the level of the concepts consciously used to describe the task domain. The explanations of behavior provided at this "subsymbolic" level are like those traditional in the physical sciences and unlike those provided by symbolic or LOT models. Furthermore, to the extent that one can interpret connectionist activity in terms of specific content, interpretations may most naturally be assigned to patterns of activation over *ensembles* of units, not to features of individual units.

Proponents of the symbolic approach, however, contend that the connectionist approach to cognition is inadequate. An influential critique of connectionism is presented by Fodor and Pylyshyn (1988), who focus on the requirement of *systematicity.* They point out that the normal linguistic competence of a native speaker is systematic, in the sense that speakers who know how to say "John loves the girl" also know how to say "The girl loves John." The natural explanation for this ability is that linguistic competence involves the grasp of a compositional semantics, i.e., a way of getting meanings of whole sentences from the meanings of their subsentential parts. Fodor and Pylyshyn propose an exactly analogous argument for *thought.* Creatures who can *think* that John loves the girl can typically also think that the girl loves John. The natural explanation is that thoughts, like sentences, have constituent structure. Thinking that John loves the girl involves having some relation to an internal representational structure with proper parts standing for "John," "loves," "the," and "girl," along with some kind of combinatorial syntactic structuring. This kind of structuring is precisely what connectionism lacks, which renders it fundamentally inadequate as an approach to cognition.

Whether this critique of connectionism and defense of the symbolic approach is compelling enough (see Clark 1989 for reservations), it illustrates how the philosophy of mind has become intimately intertwined with the foundations of cognitive science.

Folk Psychology and Eliminativism

While the LOT hypothesis has been relatively controversial, the functionalist position has enjoyed a very high degree of acceptance. Recall the nine causal laws we gave as illustrations of the laws that supposedly hold among inputs, internal states, and outputs. These causal laws are said to be part of a commonsense "theory" of the mind, a theory supposedly embedded in the wisdom of the common folk. It is a theory passed on from generation to generation, learned by each child at its mother's knee. Since it resembles a theory of scientific psychology, it is often referred to as *folk psychology.* The causal laws contained in folk psychology are allegedly used by ordinary people in everyday life to explain and predict behavior. For example, we might explain Sally's shopping at a certain store by saying that she decided to save as much money as possible and she believed that shopping at that store was the best way to save money. Her decision and belief explain her action when they are conjoined with law C_2.

Although numerous philosophers and psychologists agree on the existence of a folk theory of mind, there is sharp disagreement on the merits of the theory. Some writers, such as Fodor (1987), extoll the virtues of the folk theory and urge cognitive science to emulate its basic contours. Other writers view folk psychology as a dubious set of laws that will require drastic revision or outright rejection as the science of mind becomes more refined.

Paul Churchland (1981) has taken the strongest stance in the latter camp (see also Stich 1983). Churchland argues first that folk psychology is a *bad* empirical theory as judged by the usual standards of theoretical virtue. He points his finger to three putative failings. First, he says that the theory is severely limited or incomplete; there are many things it fails to explain or even to address. The nature of mental illness, the basis of intelligence differences among individuals, the function of sleep, the ability to catch an outfield fly ball on the run, and the nature of learning are all left totally mysterious within the framework of folk psychology. Second, he claims that folk psychology is stagnant and infertile. The folk psychology of the ancient Greeks is essentially the folk psychology we use today; it gives us no better a means of explaining human behavior than we had in the time of Sophocles. Such lack of progress, according to some philosophers of science (Lakatos 1970), is a mark of a poor theory. Third, folk psychology is not well integrated with the other sciences of man and beast. It alone uses "intentional" categories and invokes propositional or conceptual contents with "aboutness"; the content can even be "about" things that don't exist, like unicorns or fountains of youth. These categories are unlikely to be reducible to the categories of biology, chemistry, or neuroscience. Ultimately, this framework is apt to be jettisoned by a science of behavior, just as alchemy and the Aristotelian cosmology were ultimately jettisoned. In other words, Churchland expects folk psychology to be replaced by a scientific psychology with rather different constructs. If and when this occurs, the distinctive folk psychological constructs, viz., the propositional attitudes, will suffer the same fate as phlogiston, caloric, and the notions of other superseded empirical theories: They will be eliminated.

Churchland's version of eliminativism is still another version of materialism. Unlike type-type materialism, however, which admits the existence of propositional attitudes and hopes to identify each attitude with some sort of neural property, eliminativism denies that there are any propositional attitudes at all. Neural events and neural properties are *all* there is. Cognitive science need not find a place for the attitudes because they simply don't exist; they are mistakenly posited by a bad (or at least suboptimal) theory. In Churchland's hands, then, a large family of mental states that are widely cited in ordinary conversation as causes of people's behavior is rejected outright.

The arguments for eliminativism are open to rejoinder. Colin McGinn (1989) replies to Churchland as follows. First, the charge of explanatory incompleteness does not prove the falsity of folk psychology; it only proves that folk psychology doesn't contain the whole truth. If explanatory incompleteness provided a good enough objection to folk psychology, it would be a good enough objection to almost any scientific theory, since theories are seldom finished and complete. Second, McGinn rebuts the charge of stagnation with the contention that scientific psychology has made most progress when it has taken folk psychology seriously rather than repudiating it. It is now widely agreed (especially among cognitive scientists) that during the period of behaviorism, when the "mentalism" of commonsense psychology was rejected, scientific psychology became quite infertile. Psychology has made more progress since it began talking and theorizing in terms of information processing, symbol manipulation, tacit knowledge, and so forth. So, contrary to Churchland, infusions of folk psychology seem to have benefited psychology, not retarded it. Third, even if folk psychology cannot be reduced to lower level sciences, that doesn't mean that it cannot be integrated with them. Integration does not require reduction.

A different way to challenge eliminativism is to question its basic premise (a premise it shares with other functionally inspired approaches), viz., that people understand or define propositional attitudes in terms of a commonsense *theory.* If they do not, we cannot reject or disqualify folk psychology because of the limitations or infirmities of any such theory. Let us ask, then, whether people's understanding of the language of attitudes and of other mental terms really rests on belief in a theory—in a set of causal laws of the sort posited by functionalism.

Cognitive Science and Mental Concepts

The question before us is how an ordinary person understands the various mental words that he or she uses. According to some functionalists (whether eliminativist or realist in spirit), the ordinary speaker associates a distinctive functional role with each separate mental word (or phrase), and this association provides the person's understanding of that word. Let us call this approach *representational functionalism* because it is concerned with the way speakers *represent* their mental words. (Representational functionalism approximates what others have called "analytic" or "commonsense" functionalism.)

To define a mental state in terms of a functional role is to define it in purely relational terms. A state's functional role is identified by other states or events to which it is (or tends to be) causally related, either as effect or as (partial) cause. A functional role says nothing whatever about the intrinsic character or properties of the state. So if representational functionalism (RF) is correct, the concept that an ordinary person associates with each mental word or phrase is a purely relational concept. Is this hypothesis plausible?

Although this question arises in the context of philosophical controversy, it should really be addressed, and is being addressed, by empirical cognitive research. What we have here is a question about the concepts that are cognitively associated with mental language. This is perfectly analogous to a question about the concepts associated with other words in the language, such as "bird," "flower," or "mother." In general, problems of this sort properly belong to empirical cognitive science, because exactly what a typical speaker or hearer associates with any given lexical item is an empirical matter. What we seek, in all such cases, is a hypothesis that provides the best explanation of the speaker's or hearer's production and comprehension of the word (or phrase) in question. Such a hypothesis would have to take account of the real-time use of the word in everyday speech. Thus, the correctness or viability of RF properly falls within the domain of cognitive science, and that is the spirit in which we shall approach it. (For detailed discussion, see Goldman 1993a.)

As a general framework, the following assumption seems plausible. To have a concept of X, for any word X, is to have some sort of representation of X stored in long-term memory. This representation controls one's decisions of whether to classify a target object or state as an instance of X. People cannot usually "introspect" their concepts; in other words, we cannot count on them to reliably report what they associate with the word "chair," for example, or with such mental words as "headache," "belief," "desire," "excited," and so on. That is why RF must be treated as an empirical hypothesis. We cannot reject this hypothesis by asking people to describe these mental-word concepts and finding that they do not give us a functionalist story. Nor can we accept the functionalist hypothesis without evidence that RF is the best explanatory account of how people use mental words.

Uses of mental words include both judgments people make (or are prepared to make) about their own mental states and judgments about other people's mental states. So let us ask how people go about making such judgments. What cognitive steps or operations are plausibly involved? Since we are especially interested in RF, what story about such cognitive steps and operations would be entailed by RF, and is such a story really plausible? Let us begin with first-person cases, i.e., with self-ascriptions of mental states.

First-Person Attributions

When a person classifies a perceived object as a chair, presumably he has some active perceptual information about that object that matches his stored concept of a chair, i.e., the representation in long-term memory associated with the word "chair." (That is the general assumption behind Biederman's geon theory presented in Chapter 1.) Let us assume that the same sort of thing transpires in the case of mental classifications. If a person classifies himself as currently having a headache, or an itch, his cognitive system must have received some sort of information that matches his concept of *headache* or his concept of *itch.* If RF is right, then the concept of *headache* will be some sort of functional role specification; call it F(headache). Thus, in order for a person to self-ascribe *headache,* he (or his cognitive system) must have information about a current state of his that matches F(headache). That is, the information must embody or carry the information "F(headache) holds of one of my current states." Is it plausible that one always possesses this kind of functional information whenever one self-ascribes *headache* (whenever one either says "I have a headache" or is prepared to say this)? Not at all, I suggest.

The first problem with this thesis can be illustrated by a morning headache. Suppose I wake up in the morning with a headache and immediately classify my state as having a headache. How do I make this classification? Surely I don't do it by identifying an actual cause of the headache, since I do not have (nor does my cognitive system have) any relevant information about the headache's cause. There hasn't been time to obtain such information since awakening. Similarly, the classification cannot be based on information about any effect of the headache, because the classification may precede any effect that could be detected. Thus, there is no way my cognitive system could arrive at the belief that a current state of mine fits the specification F(headache), if this requires attention to actual causes or effects of the current (token) state.

However, all may not be lost. Perhaps a cautious version of functionalism would not imply anything about the actual causes and effects of a particular headache. Functional laws should be construed subjunctively, as specifying states that *would* be caused under given circumstances. For example, (B_2) in our list of laws should be understood as saying that if a person wanted to drink and believed that a potable liquid was in the refrigerator, then he *would* form an intention to go to the refrigerator. Thus, a token desire to drink need not *actually* cause a token intention to go to the refrigerator, because the indicated belief may not actually be present. Nonetheless, a desire to drink must have the subjunctive property of being such that *if* the indicated belief were present, then the indicated intention *would* ensue.

To solve the morning-headache problem, then, an RF theorist might hypothesize that I classify my state as a headache by detecting an appropriate subjunctive property. What I have detected is that the current state is of a kind that would cause me to take aspirin if aspirin were around and I knew (believed) where it was. But this suggestion immediately introduces the second problem: How can such a subjunctive property of a current state be detected? How does one determine that a target state is the sort of state that would produce a certain action under the specified circumstances unless it actually produces this action? In standard cases, subjunctive beliefs about particular objects are inferred from categorical premises about those objects, typically premises about an intrinsic, nonrelational property of the object in question. For example, I conclude that a specific white lump would dissolve if it were immersed in water because I believe it is a piece of sugar and that sugar is soluble. But what is the analogous categorical and intrinsic property I detect about the headache that permits the subjunctive conclusion?

The third problem, the threat of combinatorial explosion, arises from the fact that functional roles for most mental-state concepts involve relations to other mental states. That is, they involve S-S relations. A particular mental state qualifies as a desire to drink, for example, only if it would produce various further desires or intentions if it were accompanied by suitable beliefs, e.g., it would produce an intention to grasp a nearby glass and bring it to my lips if I believed such a glass were within reach. The problem, however, is that these further desires or intentions must themselves be classified (type-identified) by means of their own relationships to other internal states. Thus, to identify a given state as an instance of type F_1, I need to identify its (actual or subjunctive) internal relata, say F_2, F_3, and F_4. But to identify something as F_2, I need to identify *its* relata as, say, F_{20}, F_{21}, and F_{22}. And so forth. This procedure is not necessarily a vicious regress, because at some point there are "exits" from the internal states to input and output events. But evidently the computational requirements of continuing this process until suitable "exits" are reached are very great. It seems extremely doubtful that our cognitive system performs these computations about a state's relata in the time it actually takes to execute self-ascriptions of mental states. This line of reasoning is not a decisive disproof of RF, of course, but it poses very serious questions indeed.

To solve the second and third problems, the RF theorist might grant that the cognitive system uses information about the *intrinsic* (nonrelational) and *categorical* (nondispositional) properties of a target state, just as one infers the solubility of a particular cube from its possession of the intrinsic and categorical properties of sugar. But which intrinsic and categorical properties might be detected in the case of mental states?

The best candidates, it would seem, are so-called *qualitative* properties of mental states—their phenomenological or subjective *feelings* (often called "qualia"). Certainly it is highly plausible that one classifies such sensations as headaches or itches on the basis of their qualitative feel. (The only other intrinsic and categorical properties of mental states would seem to be neural properties. But these are not generally known or detected by the ordinary cognizer, or even by the cognitive system, and are therefore not such good candidates. For further discussion, see Goldman 1993a.) The defender of RF would now have to say that the system uses information about the qualitative character of a mental state as a *premise* to infer the target state's functional role and then matches that role to the concept representation.

Once we acknowledge the need for qualitative properties, however, we realize that we can get a much simpler model of mentalistic self-ascription by dispensing with the functional roles entirely. Why not adopt a very different model in which the concepts of headache, itch, and so forth are representations of qualitative characteristics, not functional roles at all? This new approach, of course, would require us to abandon RF, but this move seems warranted by the present considerations.

These considerations indicate that something closer to the Cartesian conception—the idea that mental concepts involve intrinsic, introspectible qualities—may have more merit than functionalists allow. Moreover, this view need not be construed as inimical or antithetical to the perspective of cognitive science. Cognitive science may itself need to postulate qualitative forms of representation. Indeed, it already seems to do so in its treatments of the sensory modalities and its talk of multiple "codes," "formats," or "media" of mental representation. Furthermore, such an account need not necessarily lead to dualism.

Whether the qualitative or phenomenological approach to mental concepts could be extended from sensations to attitudes is an open question. Even this prospect, though, is not beyond the bounds of credibility. There is no reason why phenomenological characteristics should be restricted to sensory characteristics, and it does indeed seem to "feel" a particular way to experience doubt, surprise, or disappointment, all of which are forms of propositional attitudes. (For more on this and related themes, see Goldman 1993a; Searle 1992; and Flanagan 1992.)

Third-Person Attributions

I have suggested that RF and the folk theory approach are empirically implausible when applied to the task of explaining self-ascriptions. What about third-person ascriptions? Here the approach seems very attractive. Indeed, it might seem hard to imagine how ordinary people could ascribe mental states to others without having a repertoire of causal laws from which to infer these states. If language users possessed a "theory of mind," they could use I-S laws to make "forward" inferences from, say, someone's physical environment and ocular gaze to his visual experiences or visual beliefs, and they could use S-O laws to make "backward" inferences from the person's observed behavior to his desires, plans, or intentions. (These backward inferences, admittedly, are tricky; they must be inferences to the "best explanation" of the behavior.) But how could people ascribe mental states to others if they lacked such laws? Moreover, people have a substantial degree of success in predicting the behavior of others. How could we attain such success, especially given the complexity of human behavior, unless we had mastered a substantial number of reasonably accurate laws? It seems as if the functionalist or folk theory model is utterly essential in accounting for third-person ascriptions.

A competing theory has emerged, however, in recent years, defended especially by Robert Gordon (1986, 1992), the present author (Goldman 1989, 1992c, 1992d), and Paul Harris (1989, 1992). This alternative theory proposes that people use a *simulation heuristic* to ascribe mental states to others and to predict and explain their behavior. This idea is continuous with the tradition of "Verstehen" (represented by such historical philosophers as Giambattista Vico, Johann Herder, Wilhelm Dilthey, and R. G. Collingwood), which claimed that understanding other people is primarily a matter of empathy or imaginative projection into their situation, or "putting yourself in their shoes." Psychologists have used the language of "role playing" and "perspective taking" to express this idea.

A simple example of the simulation heuristic is a tennis player's anticipation of his opponent's next shot. The player asks himself, "Where would *I* aim my next shot if I were in his position on the court and had his beliefs about his tennis skills?" Pretending to have the opponent's goals and beliefs, the simulator allows his own practical reasoning mechanisms or calculational processes to operate on these goals and beliefs to generate a choice. This (feigned) choice is then adopted as the predicted choice of the opponent.

There are three fundamental elements in the simulation model. First, the simulator must construct a pretend or feigned mental state that mirrors the state of the simulated agent as closely as possible. This construction will be based on the simulator's prior information about the agent's condition (however good or bad that information is). Second, the simulator must feed these pretend states into a cognitive process or mechanism that operates on these inputs to generate further mental states. It is assumed that the process operates on the feigned states in the same manner that it operates on actual states of the same sort. A practical reasoning process, for example, generates decisions from surrogate belief and desire inputs in the same way that it generates decisions from genuine beliefs and desires. Third, instead of acting on the generated output (e.g., the decision), the simulator takes it "offline" and uses it as a basis for attributing the output state to the agent.

The principal difference between the simulation model and the folk-theory model is that the former does not impute to the attributor any cognitive possession of causal laws that govern the practical reasoning mechanism (or whatever mechanism generates output mental states from inputs). The simulation model dispenses with the requirement that an attributor *knows* much about his own psychology or the psychology of others. It instead postulates an ability to *use* one's own psychology as a sort of *analogue device* to parallel the psychology of the other. It allows us to assume that the attributor is quite naive in matters of mental theory and lawful generalization.

The simulation heuristic is depicted in a flowchart format in Figure 3.1. This figure shows a decision-making system that normally receives inputs from belief and desire sources. It can also receive inputs, however, from a pretend belief and desire generator, as shown in the lower right-hand corner. When decisions are made in the pretend mode, they are not sent to the action control systems but are instead submitted to the belief system, there to become the subjects of beliefs about the agent's probable decisions.

Can a simulator's conclusions about an agent's mental states and behavior be accurate despite the simulator's theoretical naivete? Conclusions can be quite accurate if three conditions are met: (1) The simulator's decision-making system (or other cognitive mechanism) is sufficiently similar to the agent's; (2)

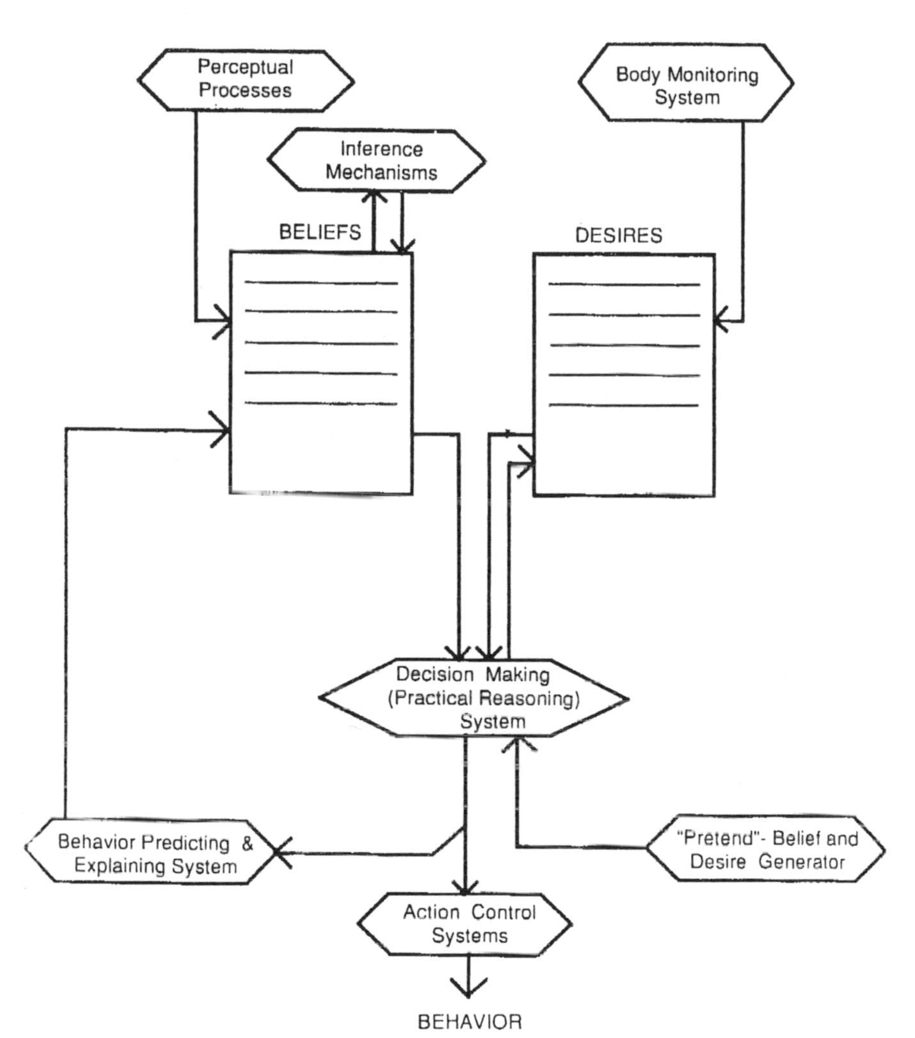

FIGURE 3.1 The simulation heuristic. *Source:* S. Stich and S. Nichols, "Folk Psychology: Simulation or Tacit Theory?" *Mind and Language* 7 (1992): 35–71. Reprinted by permission of Blackwell Publishers.

the system operates on pretend states in the same way that it operates on genuine states; and (3) the simulator generates pretend states that correspond quite faithfully to actual states of the agent. Condition 1 appears to be satisfied. At the basic psychological level, there seems to be sufficient similarity across individuals to ensure accuracy. Condition 2 is also fairly plausible. It certainly seems that the condition is met in ordinary cases of hypothetical planning, for example. I can plan to drive to a certain crosstown locale on the feigned intention of going there this afternoon in the same way that I can plan this drive when I actually have that intention. Similarly, in the course of examining a scientific hypothesis, I can reason from a pretend belief in this hypothesis in the same way I would reason from a genuine belief in it. Condition 3, however, is not always met; its degree of satisfaction is variable. That is perfectly all right, however. The simulation theory does not claim that people are always good simulators or accurate predictors of others' actions. Their accuracy is quite variable and indeed depends on the degree to which they faithfully simulate the actual initial states of the agents. In general, people have special difficulty in projecting themselves into the position of people "alien" to themselves, e.g., those of another culture, generation, or gender. Even in the case of fairly similar people, simulators may lack specific information about an agent's tastes and life experience that is essential for accurate simulation.

The Theory Theory Versus the Simulation Theory

The folk-theory model, or "theory theory," and the simulation model offer rival accounts of the ascription of mental states to others (although one can admit partial realization of each). Which one is correct is a matter to be settled by the empirical methods of cognitive science. Little has been done thus far to compare their merits, partly because the simulation theory is a new entry in the field and most practitioners have simply assumed that something like the folk-theory model must be correct. However, let us examine some evidence in the developmental and clinical fields and see how well the rival theories can accommodate them.

The most discussed evidence in the developmental field is the finding by Heinz Wimmer and Josef Perner (1983) that, between three and five years of age, children undergo a marked improvement in their ability to ascribe false beliefs to others. In one experiment, children see a puppet named Maxi put his chocolate in a box and go out to play. Next they see his mother transfer the chocolate to the cupboard while Maxi is still out. Where will Maxi look for the chocolate when he returns? A five-year-old says that he will look in the box, a response typical of an adult. But the child of three indicates the cupboard, the place where the three-year-old himself believes it to be. The three-year-old has not yet mastered the art of belief ascription, but the five-year-old has.

This result might also be taken to show that the three-year-old has not yet mastered the "theory of mind" while the five-year-old has mastered it quite well. This interpretation favors the folk-theory approach. But the result can equally be accommodated by the simulation theory. So, at least, it is argued by Paul Harris (1992). Harris traces a sequence of four developmental stages that normal children traverse, based on a range of empirical findings. He then shows how a development of simulation ability could accommodate these stages just as well as a development in the theory of mind. On the simulation approach, a crucial phase of the development would be characterized by an increase in *imaginative* power. The younger children (e.g., three-year-olds) have a hard time imagining a belief that runs directly counter to what they currently take to be the case, whereas the older children have the ability to feign a state in another person that directly conflicts with their own current state.

Drawing on the Wimmer-Perner results, some fascinating related work has been done with autistic children. Autistic children are of special interest because they are particularly weak at reciprocal social interaction, having qualitative impairments in both verbal and nonverbal communication. They are sometimes described as having an impairment at "mentalizing." This impairment was confirmed in an experiment by Simon Baron-Cohen, Alan Leslie, and Uta Frith (1985) in which autistic children with a mean age of about twelve years displayed precisely the same sort of response in false-belief tasks as three-year-olds. By contrast, Down's syndrome children whose general mean IQ was no higher than that of the autistic children generally answered the false-belief question correctly. These findings strongly suggest that autism may involve a specific cognitive deficit pertaining to mentalizing.

This leaves open, however, whether the normal mentalizing faculty involves a functionalist-style theory or whether it involves the use of the simulation heuristic. One intriguing fact that ostensibly supports the latter is that autistic children also show a deficiency in pretend play. Maybe this deficiency is associated with underdevelopment of their simulational powers.

In a second study, Baron-Cohen, Leslie, and Frith (1986) gave autistic children scrambled pictures from comic strips. They were supposed to put the pictures in proper order to make up a story, and then tell the story in their own words. There were three types of stories: mechanical, behavioral, and mentalistic. The autistic children performed quite well on the mechanical and behavioral stories but very poorly on the mentalistic ones. They put the pictures of this type in a jumbled order and told their stories without attribution of mental states. (Nonautistic children, by comparison, performed better than autistic children on the mentalistic stories, equally well on the behavioral ones, and less well on the mechanical stories.)

The fact that autistic children do well on the mechanical and behavioral scripts suggests that they have no impairment in theorizing or making theoretical inferences. This finding initially seems to count against the theory theory and to support the simulation approach. The results are not conclusive, however, since proponents of the theory theory may grant that autistic children have no *general* impairment in theorizing capacity, only in the *special-purpose* theorizing associated with mentalizing. It is noteworthy, however, that autistic children are also known to be very weak at empathizing.

Stephen Stich and Shaun Nichols (1992) prefer the theory approach over the simulation approach because implicit theories must be postulated in other areas of cognitive competence, such as grammar and naive physics. The simulation theorist may reply, however, that the significance of simulation, or role taking, is also well established in other areas, e.g., in empathic arousal. In a study by Stotland (1969), subjects were instructed to imagine how they would feel and what sensations they would have in their hands if they were exposed to the same painful heat treatment that was being applied to another person. These subjects gave more evidence of empathic distress than (1) subjects instructed to attend closely to the other person's physical movements and (2) subjects instructed to imagine how the other person felt when he or she was undergoing the treatment.

There is much empirical work to be done before a clear choice can be made between the theory theory and the simulation theory. Chapter 5 reviews additional evidence in support of the simulation theory in the context of a discussion of empathy-based motivation. What should be stressed here, however, is that the choice between the theory theory and the simulation theory and other conclusions about how ordinary people understand mental states should ultimately be made on empirical grounds. These questions cannot be resolved by a priori speculation but must take account of research in cognitive science.

The dispute between the theory theory and the simulation theory bears important implications for the metaphysical issues in the philosophy of mind. If the theory theory is correct and people's understanding of mental state concepts essentially involves tacit acceptance of a folk theory, then the eliminativist has a foot in the door. He can proceed to argue (however persuasively) that the folk theory is a poor theory and that its constructs do not pick out genuine states of the mind-brain. If the simulation theory is correct, however, people's ascriptions of mental states to others can be explained without assuming they follow the principles of a large-scale folk theory. This conclusion would undercut the initial premise of the eliminativist argument and help support a realist approach to mental states and propositional attitudes. In this fashion, empirical findings in psychology and philosophical problems again turn out to be interrelated.

Suggestions for Further Reading

Philosophy of mind has an enormous literature. The suggestions that follow are highly selective, based on accessibility, prominence, or pertinence to cognitive science. There are several good general anthologies in the philosophy of mind: Lycan (1990), Rosenthal (1991), Beakley and Ludlow (1992), and Block (1980). Good single-authored surveys include P. M. Churchland (1988b), Bechtel (1988), and Sterelny (1990).

Early formulations of functionalism by Putnam, Lewis, and others are reprinted in Lycan (1990), Rosenthal (1991), and Block (1980), as well as [R]. Recent defenses of functionalism include Lycan (1987) and Pollock (1989).

Major discussions of the problem of intentionality and mental content include Fodor (1981, 1987, 1990), Davidson (1984), Dennett (1978, 1987), Stich (1983), Searle (1983), Millikan (1984), and Dretske (1988). For a brief critical survey, see Cummins (1989); for a more complex critical appraisal, see Schiffer (1987). Several of these authors are represented by selections in [R].

The connectionist approach to cognitive science is explained and assessed in such works as Clark (1989) [R], P. M. Churchland (1989), Bechtel and Abrahamsen (1991), and Horgan and Tienson (1991).

Discussions of consciousness and qualia loom large in current controversies. See Dennett (1991) [R], Flanagan (1992), Searle (1992), Harman (1990), and Block (1990).

The debate between the theory theory and the simulation theory spans both philosophy and developmental psychology. A good sample of the debate appears in a double issue of the journal *Mind and Language* (7:1/2, 1992) devoted to the simulation theory. These and other articles on the simulation theory are reprinted in Davies and Stone (1993). Work in developmental psychology on the child's theory of mind appears in Astington, Harris, and Olson (1988), Wellman (1990), and Perner (1991). Gopnik (1993) [R] and Goldman (1993a) [R] take opposing positions on the theory theory.

Chapter Four

Metaphysics

Descriptive and Prescriptive Metaphysics

Metaphysics is usually characterized as the branch of philosophy that asks: (1) What exists? and (2) For each existent, what is its nature or "mode of being"? Metaphysicians obviously do not want a list of every individual thing that exists; rather, they are interested in the different *types* of entities that populate the world. For example, they want to know if numbers are among the things that exist. If so, what is their nature. Similarly, metaphysicians do not seek an itemization of all causal interactions in the universe (obviously a fruitless quest). But they do want to know if there are genuine causal relations between events and, if so, to understand the nature of such relations.

Questions of metaphysics are often sparked by common beliefs or expressions of language. For example, people naively believe in the persistence or continued existence of objects over time. You probably assume that one and the same telephone has been in your office (or home) throughout an entire year and that you yourself have continued to exist as one and the same individual from the time of your birth. People also appear to believe in the existence of "possibilities," as evidenced by such statements as "There is a possibility of rain this evening."

One way of studying metaphysics, then, is to examine the kinds of entities and properties to which our common beliefs and language are committed. To be sure, if the metaphysician wants to inquire into what "really" exists and examine its "true" nature, uncritical reliance on ordinary beliefs and everyday language may be misplaced. Perhaps the discoveries of science and the scrutiny of philosophical reflection will detect errors and confusions in ordinary thought. But the ontology of prereflective thought and language—*folk ontology,* we might call it—seems to be a good place to begin. Let us call an inquiry that simply tries to portray or reconstruct our folk ontology *descriptive metaphysics,* and let us call an inquiry that tries to limn the genuine nature of reality, however far removed from the commonsensical vision of the world, *prescriptive metaphysics.* Both branches of metaphysics deserve attention; furthermore, as we shall see, both branches can benefit from contributions by cognitive science.

Beginning with descriptive metaphysics, we immediately confront a problem. When we speak of "our" ordinary ontological commitments or existential beliefs, to whom does "our" refer? The entire human race? If so, we must presuppose that all people share the same ontological beliefs. But is there really a single, uniform folk ontology? To the contrary, aren't there dramatic differences between ontological views across different cultures and even among different individuals within a single culture? Some believe in the existence of God and others reject any deity. Belief in witches was widespread in the sixteenth century but is comparatively infrequent today. Whose set of ontological posits, then, should descriptive metaphysics seek to uncover?

Descriptive metaphysics, however, is not so interested in the local and highly variable beliefs and conceptions that mark differences among cultures. Rather, it is chiefly, if not exclusively, interested in fundamental ontological conceptions, particularly those that are universal to (mature) human beings as such. It is still an open question, of course, whether there are any universal ontological conceptions. Certain forms of cultural relativism would dispute their very existence. So descriptive metaphysics must first undertake to decide whether universal ontological conceptions exist in the first place. If this preliminary question is answered in the affirmative, descriptive metaphysics can then proceed to delineate the detailed contents of these ontological views. Both problems are ones that cognitive science can help us address.

Physical Bodies

An obvious candidate for a universal conception is the conception of physical objects. The philosopher Willard van Orman Quine (1973) has remarked that people are "body-minded" creatures, in the sense that the units into which they intuitively divide or segment the world are entities like rocks, trees, and snakes. By contrast, if we describe to people a random conglomeration of spatially separated elements, such as a-rock-and-a-tree-and-the Eiffel-Tower, they do not find this sort of thing a natural unit or "object" at all. Consider an example of Eli Hirsch (1982). If two people, A and B, are in physical contact exclusively with each other during an interval of time, we can define an entity called a *cperson* whose history consists of person A before the contact, person B during the contact interval, and person A again after the interval. Hirsch calls this a "strange" kind of entity because everybody would regard it as a bizarre or unnatural unit, not a single object at all.

It appears, then, that people prefer an ontology that excludes such things as cpersons or rock-tree-Eiffel-Tower conglomerations, and descriptive metaphysics is concerned with reporting such facts. Two other types of questions should further occupy descriptive metaphysics. First, what implicit criteria or principles of unity determine people's intuitive preference for one set of objects rather than another? There seem to be principles of both *spatial* and *temporal* unity that bind elements into intuitive wholes. What exactly are these unity principles? Second, what is the source of these unity principles? Does it reside in features of language, which could easily diverge across languages and cultures? Or is there a single biologically based conception of physical bodies shared by all people?

Questions about principles of unity have been discussed since ancient times. A famous example concerns the Ship of Theseus. Suppose the planks of this ship, as they got old and warped, were replaced until gradually all of the ship's planks were replaced by new ones. Is it still the same ship as it was initially? That is, is the later ship—call it S_2— identical to the original ship—S_1? To make the case harder, suppose that the old planks were thrown into a junkyard as they were removed from the ship and that much later someone took these original planks and reassembled them anew. Is this newly assembled ship—called S_3—the same as the original ship, S_1? Or is S_2 still the same as S_1? (Presumably they can't both be identical with S_1.) This example raises the question of what is crucial to identity or unity over time: having the same material parts, or such factors as continuity versus discontinuity over time?

As we have said, descriptive metaphysics is interested in discovering what principles tacitly underpin people's intuitive judgments about unity. In the Ship of Theseus case, most people are intuitively inclined to identify S_2 (rather than S_3) with S_1. This answer suggests that continuity over time is a more important principle than material composition. Continuity also seems to be an important factor in spatial unity, as the unnaturalness of the rock-and-tree-and-Eiffel-Tower example suggests. Specifying such principles in detail is one of the tasks of descriptive metaphysics.

Both Quine and Hirsch have pointed out that the problem of spatial unity was in effect addressed by the Gestalt psychologists, who studied the principles of object unity as they are manifested in perceptual organization. Working in the early part of this century, the Gestalt psychologists proposed principles that are descriptively quite successful, at least for adult perceivers. The founder of Gestalt psychology, Max Wertheimer (1923), claimed that there are several unlearned factors used in perceptual grouping or organization, including (1) proximity, (2) similarity, (3) good continuation, and (4) closure. The principle of proximity says that the closer two figures are to each other, the more they will tend to be grouped together, or unified, perceptually. In Figure 4.1a, the six lines will generally be perceived as three pairs of lines. The principle of similarity says that, other things equal, we group similar elements together. Thus, in Figure 4.1b, we group filled-in circles with other filled-in circles and empty circles with empty circles. As a result, we see columns in the first case and rows in the second case. The principle of good continuation says that the visual system prefers contours that continue smoothly along their original course. Thus in Figure 4.1c, segment A will be grouped (or unified) with D and segment C with B. The fourth principle, closure, says that we tend to "complete" figures that have gaps in them. Figure 4.1d is seen as a triangle despite the fact that the sides are incomplete.

The principles are not really confined to the visual modality or to synchronic as opposed to diachronic unity. Proximity operates in time just as it does in space, as in the case of auditory rhythms. Four drumbeats with a pause between the second and third are heard as two pairs: the first and second as one phrasal unit and the third and fourth as another.

According to Gestalt psychology, then, people have built-in principles of organization that jointly compose or determine their conception of object unity. However, while the Gestalt principles do well in accounting for adult patterns of object organization, recent work in developmental psychology, especially by Elizabeth Spelke and her coworkers, raises doubts about the applicability of these principles to infants.

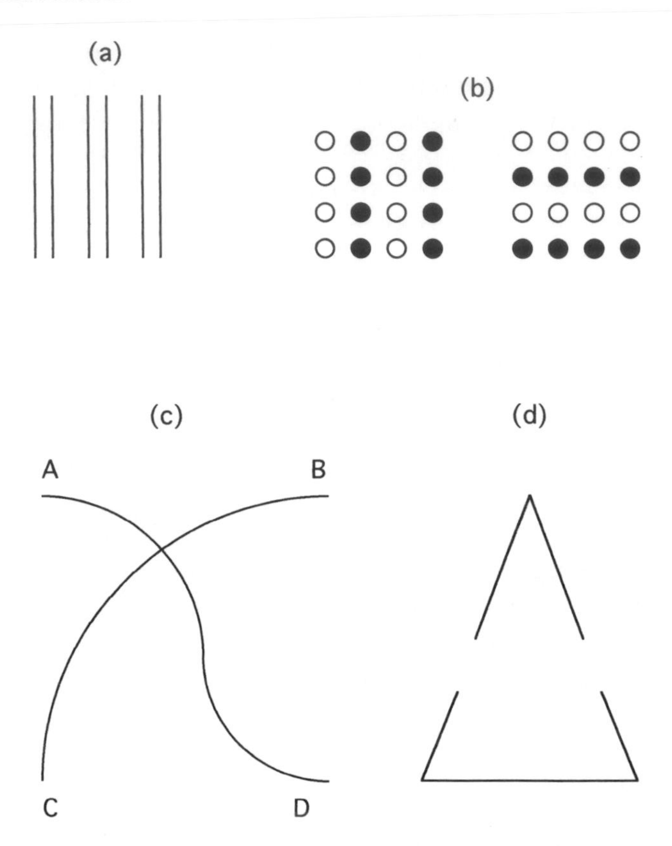

FIGURE 4.1 Illustrations of Gestalt principles of figural goodness.

Before presenting Spelke's findings, we need to be reminded (from Chapter 2) of the experimental methodology used in studying young infants. This method is based on the phenomenon of *habituation,* in which regularly repeated stimuli, like the tick of a clock, gradually fade from attention and consciousness. R. L. Fantz (1961) applied this well-known phenomenon to the study of perceptual capacities in infancy. He found that when young infants are presented repeatedly with the same visual display, they tend to look at it less and less. If the infants are then presented both with the original display and a new display, they tend to look longer at the new display. This preference indicates that infants can discriminate between the two displays and detect the novelty of the second one. Spelke has used this procedure to study the extent to which Gestalt principles are operative at various ages, and to determine if other principles of object unity may be at work instead (see Spelke 1990a, 1990b).

If infants had the same perceptual properties as adults, then they would "complete" the shape of a stationary object that was occluded or hidden at its center by a nearer object, like the triangle in Figure 4.1d. To test this hypothesis, four-month-old infants were allowed to look at length at simple shapes that were center-occluded. Then they were allowed to look either at the complete figure or at the fragmented elements, as presented schematically in Figure 4.2. It turned out that infants did not show any preference between those displays. Infants also did not seem responsive to the factor of similarity or dissimilarity. Two adjacent motionless objects that differed in color, texture, and shape were not perceived as distinct. These experiments provide evidence that infants do not perceive the unity of objects according to the Gestalt principles of analyzing the static, configurational properties of visual arrays.

However, Spelke found evidence that infants use a number of other principles to determine object unity. If two objects are separated in depth, infants perceive them as distinct. Infants also detect object boundaries by relative motions of surfaces: Two objects are perceived as distinct if they move independently, even if they touch throughout their motion. Third, infants determine object identity or distinctness by analyzing the spatiotemporal continuity of motion. When object motion is apparently discontinuous, infants perceive two objects; when it is apparently continuous, they perceive one ob-

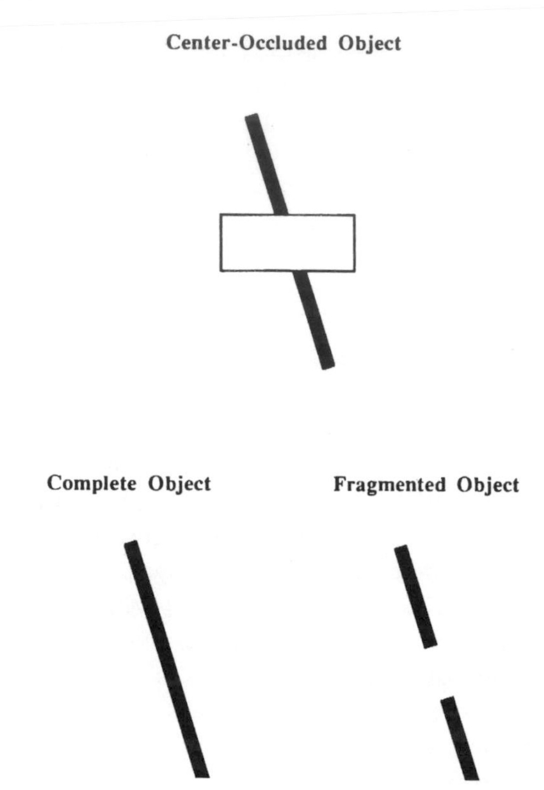

FIGURE 4.2 Habituation display (top) and test displays (bottom) for an experiment on infants' perceptions of partly occluded objects. *Source:* After P. J. Kellman and E. S. Spelke, "Perception of Partly Occluded Objects in Infancy," *Cognitive Psychology* 15 (1983): 483–524. Reprinted by permission of Academic Press.

ject. For example, four-month-old infants were habituated to events in which one or two objects moved in and out of view behind one or two occluders. When the path of object motion was apparently continuous, infants apprehended the presence of a single object leaving and returning to the field of view. When the path of motion was apparently discontinuous, infants perceived two objects, each moving continuously through part of the scene.

These and other findings led Spelke to propose four principles by which infants determine object unities: cohesion, boundedness, rigidity, and no action at a distance. According to the cohesion principle, for example, two surface points in the visual field are taken to lie on the same object only if the points are linked by a path of connected surface points. When two surfaces are separated by a spatial gap or undergo relative motions that alter the adjacency relations among points at their border, the surfaces are interpreted as lying on distinct objects.

In another series of studies, Spelke and coworkers investigated object perception in the tactile mode to see whether infants perceive the unity and boundaries of objects under the same conditions when they feel objects as when they see them. Four-month-old infants held two spatially separated rings, one in each hand, under a cloth that blocked their view of the rings and of the space between them. In different conditions, the rings could either be moved rigidly together or independently (see Figure 4.3). The infants perceived the two rings as a single unit that extended between their hands if the rings could only be moved rigidly together, but they perceived the rings as two distinct objects separated by a gap if the rings could be moved independently. Perception was unaffected by the static configurational properties of the ring displays such as similarity or dissimilarity of substance, texture, or shape. Thus, the same fundamental principles (but not the Gestalt principles) appear to be at work in the tactile, or haptic, modality as in the visual modality. In fact, Spelke hypothesizes that the mechanisms of object segmentation may be amodal, that is, located centrally in the brain and operating on inputs from either sensory modality.

In other experiments, Spelke has found that the Gestalt organizational phenomena are acquired gradually, perhaps between the ages of six months and two years. Thus, her picture is that infants have an unlearned conception of physical bodies

Rigid Motion Independent Motion

FIGURE 4.3 Apparatus for an experiment on haptic perception of object unity and boundaries. *Source:* A. Streri and E. S. Spelke, "Haptic Perception of Objects in Infancy," *Cognitive Psychology* 20 (1988): 1–23. Reprinted by permission of Academic Press.

and that the Gestalt constraints are a learned augmentation of this initial conception. The initial conception, moreover, is one that is fully present in adults as well. We do not readily consider something as a physical body if it lacks cohesion (a pile of leaves), lacks bounds (a drop of water in a pool), or lacks continuity (a row of flashing lights). These may be considered collections of objects or parts of objects, but they are not unitary and independent objects for us.

Since all of this research involves prelinguistic infants, it is clear that a basic conception of physical objects is not dependent on language (nor on culture). Thus, there does indeed appear to be a universal human conception of physical bodies as well as a universal belief in their existence.

Categories of Thought

In the history of philosophy, Kant is famous for postulating a set of categories of thought that are universal and indeed essential for cognition. In contemporary cognitive science, one of the few theorists who has tackled this kind of problem is

Ray Jackendoff. In a series of books (Jackendoff 1983, 1987, 1990) Jackendoff proposes that the conceptual structures attainable by human beings are characterized by a finite set of conceptual well-formedness rules. He takes these rules to be universal and innate and posits that everyone has essentially the same capacity to develop concepts, though the specific concepts one develops depend on experience. Furthermore, Jackendoff claims that a small number of ontological categories—such as *thing, place,* and *event*—are all present as primitives of a certain level of mental representation, which he calls *conceptual structure.* The conceptual well-formedness rules allow for conceptual constituents to develop in each of these ontological categories and provide an algebra of relationships among them specifying, for example, that a thing can occupy a place, an event may have a certain number of things and places as parts, and so forth.

The evidence Jackendoff adduces for his ontologico-conceptual hypotheses is mostly linguistic in nature. One circumstance in which a speaker clearly indicates an ontological commitment to an entity is when he refers to it by means of a demonstrative, as in (4. 1).

(4.1) That [pointing] is a dog.

The use of the demonstrative pronoun here is accompanied by a gesture that serves as an invitation to the hearer to locate the entity in his own visual field. Such a demonstrative pronoun is called a "pragmatic anaphor"; it takes its reference from nonlinguistic context. What is significant is that pragmatic anaphora is possible not only to designate objects, as in (4.1), but also entities classifiable as places (4.2a), paths or trajectories (4.2b), actions (4.2c), events (4.2d), sounds (4.2e), manners (4.2f), amounts (4.2g), and numbers (4.2h).

(4.2)(a) Your hat is here [pointing].

(b) He went thataway [pointing].
(c) Can you do that [pointing]?
Can you do this [demonstrating]?
(d) That [pointing] had better not happen in *my* house!
(e) That [gesturing] sounds like Brahms.
(f) You shuffle cards like this [demonstrating].
(g) The fish that got away was yay [demonstrating] long.
(h) Please bring back this many cookies [holding up some number of fingers] (Jackendoff 1987, 149).

The conditions on the interpretation of "that" in (4.1) also obtain with the pragmatic anaphors in (4.2). For instance, if the hearer is unable to see or figure out what goings-on the speaker is pointing at in (4.2d), he will not fully understand the utterance.

Other grammatical constructions support a similar range of entities, Jackendoff argues. For example, all of the indicated ontological categories permit the formation of a *wh*-question.

(4.3)(a) What did you buy? (Thing)
(b) Where is my coat? (Place)
(c) Where (which way) did they go? (Direction)
(d) What did you do? (Action)
(e) What happened next? (Event)
(f) How did you cook the eggs? (Manner)
(g) How long was the fish? (Amount)
(h) How many people were at the party? (Number)

Jackendoff argues that these and other types of grammatical parallels support the conclusion that expressions other than noun phrases can be used referentially and hence carry ontological commitment.

Jackendoff next seeks to show how the small number of primitive ontological categories are deployed in a variety of semantic domains. Following Gruber (1965), he suggests that spatial concepts are generalized to several other domains. (A similar thesis is advanced by Lakoff and Johnson 1980.) Consider the English verbs of *spatial position*. These can be divided into three classes, which Jackendoff calls GO verbs, BE verbs, and STAY verbs. The sentences in (4.4) exemplify the class of GO verbs.

(4.4)(a) The dog ran from the door to the table.
(b) A meteor hurtled toward the earth.
(c) The hawk flew over the prairie (Jackendoff 1987, 152).

In each sentence the object in motion, called the *theme*, travels along a path. Thus the sentences express specialized forms of the concept [GO (X, P)], which represents the motion of object X along some path P. This concept belongs to the ontological category [EVENT]: It is something that happens over time. BE verbs are exemplified in (4.5).

(4.5)(a) Max was in Africa.
(b) The cushion lay on the couch.
(c) The statue stands in the woods (153).

These verbs describe not motion but the location of an object. Thus, they express forms of the concept [BE (X, L)], where X is the theme (the object being located) and L is a location. The ontological category of this concept is not [EVENT], but [STATE].

A second class of location verbs, which Jackendoff calls STAY verbs, including "stay" and "remain," also express the location of an object in a place. But unlike BE verbs, they involve the maintenance of this location over a period of time; they cannot be attributed to a point in time such as "at six o'clock."

The verbs considered thus far are all verbs of spatial position. Next Jackendoff asks us to consider another semantic field: verbs of *possession.* These verbs can be divided into three subfields, just like the spatial position verbs.

(4.6)(a) Harry gave the book to Betty.
(b) Charlie bought the lamp from Max.
(4.7)(a) The book belonged to the library.
(b) Max owned an iguana.
(4.8)(a) The library kept the book.
(b) The iguana stayed in Max's possession (154).

The things described in (4.6) undergo a change in possession and belong to the category [EVENT]; the things described in (4.7) are in a [STATE] of possession; and the things described in (4.8) are in states of unchanging possession. Thus, we can think of the verbs in (4.6) as instances of [GO (X, P)], the verbs in (4.7) as instances of [BE (X, L)], and the verbs in (4.8) as instances of [STAY (X, L)]. The difference is that the earlier verbs were all in the semantic field of spatial position, whereas these are all in the semantic field of possession. So it is intuitively plausible that the second class of verbs is derived and understood by means of (metaphorical) extension or generalization from the first class, verbs of spatial domain.

Jackendoff next conjectures that verbs of *identification* also derive from a cross-field generalization. For example, (4.9) contains three verbs of identification, one expressing change, one expressing a state, and the third expressing persistence of a state. These sentences are again instances of the concepts GO, BE, and STAY, respectively, where the field is identificational rather than positional or possessional.

(4.9)(a) The metal turned red.
(b) The metal was vermilion.
(c) The metal stayed red (155).

As further evidence for his conjecture, Jackendoff observes that it is common for particular verbs to function in more than one semantic field while still preserving their classification as GO, BE, or STAY verbs. Here are some examples.

(4.10)(a) The coach turned into a driveway. (Positional)
The coach turned into a pumpkin. (Identificational)
(b) The train went to Texas. (Positional)
The inheritance went to Philip. (Possessional)
(c) Max is in Africa. (Positional)
Max is a dog. (Identificational)
(d) Bill kept the book on the shelf. (Positional)
Bill kept the book. (Possessional)
(e) The coach remained in the driveway. (Positional)
The coach remained a pumpkin. (Identificational)
(156).

These are intriguing illustrations of Jackendoff's thesis that our system of concepts is built up from a relatively small number of conceptual primitives together with an algebra of relationships. If descriptive metaphysics aims to characterize fundamental modes of categorizing the world, his work is clearly a contribution to descriptive metaphysics.

Prescriptive Metaphysics

Let us turn now to examples of prescriptive metaphysics. This branch of metaphysics is not simply concerned with a description or reconstruction of folk ontology; rather, it seeks to provide a *proper* ontology; one sensitive to the findings of science and the critical reflections of philosophy. Our folk ontology might be terribly naive and in need of radical reform or revision. Such revision might come in several different forms: (1) addition of types of entities or properties absent from folk ontology; (2) deletion of entities or properties that appear in folk ontology; and (3) modification of the "nature," or ontological status, imputed to certain types of entities, properties, or facts.

In the history of metaphysics, revisionary metaphysics has had different sources. Sometimes it was based on purely philosophical reflection, as in Plato's postulation of the forms. Sometimes it was based on scientific advances that forced us to rethink basic assumptions, such as our ordinary conceptions of space and time, for instance. Often it has been the product of a combination of developments in both science and philosophy. Here we are concerned with ways in which the findings of cognitive science may have an impact, in conjunction with philosophical reflection, on prescriptive metaphysics.

Color

The ontological status of color has been a thorny issue in philosophy since antiquity and has been particularly subject to controversy since the seventeenth century. The naive view is that colors are objective, intrinsic properties of physical objects. Red and green seem to characterize physical things, such as tomatoes and grass, quite independently of human responses. Whereas it is easy for common sense to agree that beauty is merely "in the eye of the beholder," it is at variance with common sense to suppose that the redness of a tomato or the greenness of grass is merely in the eye of the beholder.

Nonetheless, subjectivist and semi-subjectivist theories of color have been abroad for some time. Berkeley maintained "that all colors are equally apparent, and that none of those which we perceive are really inherent in any outward object" (1713). Locke did not go as far as Berkeley but also took issue with the commonsensical view of color. He held a dispositionalist view, according to which colors (and other so-called "secondary qualities") "are in truth nothing in the

Objects themselves, but Powers to produce various Sensations in us" (1694, Bk. II, Chap. 8, sec. 14). This view implies that physical objects do not have colors independently of (actual and possible) visual experiences, although physical objects do have dispositions to produce these experiences. This is what I call a "semi-subjectivist" position.

Locke's view was partly influenced by the physics of his day. Modern theories of color are likewise influenced by today's science, including both the physics of light and the psychophysiology of color vision (which I subsume under cognitive science). Indeed, the contemporary scientific understanding of color and color vision makes it particularly difficult to accept a purely objectivist view of color.

Color experience has three dimensions: hue, brightness, and saturation. Here we focus on hue. (My exposition substantially follows that of Gleitman 1981.) The raw material with which the visual system begins is light of various intensities and wavelengths. Since we can discriminate among different wavelengths, there must be different receptors that are differentially attuned to this physical dimension. The human visual system is *trichromatic*, which means that it contains only three different kinds of color elements, called *cones*. Each of these three cone types is a broad-band receptor, that is, each responds to a very broad range of wavelengths in the visible spectrum (i.e., the span of light waves from about 400 to 700 nanometers, where one nanometer equals one millionth of a millimeter). The main difference between the cone elements lies in their sensitivity curves. Although the overlap between the sensitivity curves is so extensive that any wavelength must necessarily stimulate each of the three receptor elements, these receptor elements respond in differing degrees depending on the wavelength. One cone type is most sensitive to wavelengths in the short-wave region of the spectrum, the second to medium wavelengths, and the third to the longer wavelengths. Thus, each wavelength produces a different ratio of the outputs of the three receptor types. Since the nervous system can tell which receptor type is sending which message, wavelength discrimination follows.

Although our receptor system allows wavelength discrimination, it is not always able to discriminate between wavelength *mixtures.* The receptor output produced by a single wavelength can be duplicated by an appropriate ("additive") mixture of wavelengths. Speaking generally, any given wavelength can be matched by the mixture of no more than three suitably balanced others. The color receptors behave like an integrator, like an adding machine that records total sums without keeping track of the component figures. This process gives rise to the phenomenon of *metamerism,* in which dramatically different wavelength combinations all produce equivalent hue experiences.

Many other properties of color experience are the products of the *opponent-processing system,* according to the generally accepted theory of Leo Hurvich and Dorothea Jameson (1957). Six different neural processes are organized into three opponent-process pairs: red-green, blue-yellow, and black-white. The two members of each pair are antagonists, so that excitation of one member automatically inhibits the other. The black-white pair does not contribute to hue, so hue experience depends on the red-green and blue-yellow pairs. Each pair can be likened to a balance: If one arm goes down, the other comes up. The hue we see depends upon the positions of the two arms.

Suppose, for example, that the red-green scale is tipped toward red and the blue-yellow scale toward yellow (excitation of red and yellow with concomitant inhibition of green and blue). Then the perceived hue is orange. If either of the two scales is evenly balanced, it makes no contribution to the hue experience. This balance occurs when neither of the two antagonists is stimulated or when both are stimulated equally and cancel each other out.

This system gives rise, for one thing, to *unique* hues, that is, hues that are seen as "pure," e.g., a blue that has no trace of red or green, or a green that has no trace of blue or yellow. This characteristic of color experience is an artifact of the opponent-processing system. For instance, a unique yellow may be evoked by stimulating the eye with monochromatic light of 580 nm, for this is the point at which neither red nor green is stimulated. But unique yellow may be equally evoked by a suitable mixture of 540 nm and 670 nm. Seen separately, 540 nm is a yellowish green and 670 nm a slightly yellowish red. The mixture has 580 nm as its dominant wavelength, even though it has no 580 nm constituent. Any light with a wavelength between 520 and 580 nm can be made to look uniquely yellow by injecting the proper amount of red to cancel the greenness, and any light above 580 nm can similarly be made to look uniquely yellow by canceling the redness with an appropriate amount of green. (See Hardin 1988, 44–45.)

This entire picture of our internal color coding system makes it difficult to interpret our color experience, upon reflection, as anything but a highly idiosyncratic artifact of that system. The division of the hues into categories, whether broad or narrow, does not seem to correspond very naturally to anything in the physical stimuli. These findings make it hard to sustain our naive, objectivist view of color; at a minimum, we seem pushed toward a dispositional or semi-subjectivist position. A color such as yellow, it seems, simply exhibits a disposition to produce a certain (range of) color experience in us.

David Hilbert (1987) tries to defend an objectivist view nonetheless. He claims that the color of a physical object is identical to its surface spectral reflectance (SSR), which is the fraction of incident light at each wavelength that the surface will reflect. Since an object's SSR is a purely physical property, this identification would make color an objective property. But the phenomenon of metamerism raises difficulties.

Objects with wildly different SSRs can all appear to be the same shade, e.g., the same shade of yellow. Hilbert is forced to maintain that such objects in fact have different colors although no normal observer is able to discriminate between them in ordinary lighting conditions. Is this theory plausible? It should be emphasized that metamerism is not just a matter of imperceptibly small differences in the wavelengths. Some metameric colors differ grossly in the percentages of light they reflect in different parts of the visible spectrum.

Hilbert replies by saying that a shade of yellow is not a particular color but a *kind* of color, that is, a *set* of SSRs. Which SSRs? Recall that objects that reflect the same amounts of light in each of the three wavebands, short, middle, and long, will appear to have the same color. Thus, following Edwin Land (1977), the common property shared by the reflectances of such objects can be expressed by summing the reflectances of the objects over each of the three ranges. This procedure yields what is called a *triplet of integrated reflectances.* Each member of this triplet expresses the reflectance of the object summed over one of the bands of wavelengths corresponding to the sensitivity of one kind of photoreceptor. Triplets of integrated reflectances defined in this way prove to be very well correlated with perceived color. Objects that share the same triplet of integrated reflectances appear to have the same color in most circumstances.

Since triplets of integrated reflectances are mathematico-physical properties of objects specified independently of observers, Hilbert feels that identification of color kinds with these properties yields an objectivist (or "realist") ontology of color. But it seems clear that this way of grouping objects does not yield "natural kinds": It does not seem to "cut nature at her joints." Instead it generates a highly gerrymandered set of groupings, the rationale for which is obviously a function of human color responses. Hilbert constrasts his view with dispositionalism, but he admits that it features a strong dose of *anthropocentrism.* This anthropocentrism, though, is at variance with the intuitive, folk ontological conception that sees colors as purely natural kinds. Thus, the findings of color science push us toward a reconceptualization of color that is at least modestly, if not radically, revisionary.

Individual Essences

A popular topic in recent philosophical discussion is essentialism. For present purposes, it is useful to distinguish two types of essentialism (see Enc 1986). One of these types, which I shall call *scientific essentialism,* holds that there are natural kinds in the world such as gold, water, and organic species like tiger and lemon. These natural kinds have essences, which are typically internal structures, like the molecular composition of water, that explain the observable, superficial features of the kind. One job of science is to identify the natural kinds and their essences.

This doctrine of scientific essentialism, made popular by Hilary Putnam (1975) and Saul Kripke (1972), has stimulated research by psychologists into the development of such concepts in children. Is it only mature scientists who conceptualize objects in terms of underlying internal structures rather than superficial features? Or do even children have the notion that hidden properties of an object, specifiable only in terms of a "theory," may be more important than its readily observable characteristics? Developmentalists such as Susan Carey (1985), Frank Keil (1989), and others suggest that even children have a bent toward scientific essentialism. This research in cognitive science is a further example of descriptive metaphysics. Since our present aim, however, is to illustrate the role of cognitive science in prescriptive metaphysics, this is not the brand of essentialism I shall pursue in this section. To introduce the topic I shall pursue, a bit of background is needed.

Many metaphysicians have held that we can draw distinctions among the properties that an individual entity possesses. Some properties are possessed merely *accidentally*, whereas others are possessed *necessarily* or *essentially*. For example, although Socrates was in fact snub-nosed, he might well have lacked this property. In other words, we might have had the same person Socrates without the property of being snub-nosed. If so, then the property of being snub-nosed is one Socrates possessed merely accidentally. There seem to be other properties, though, that Socrates could not have lacked, e.g., the property of being human. Without the property of humanity, he would not have been the same individual Socrates at all. If this notion is right, being human was an essential property of Socrates, possessed by him in all "possible worlds" in which he could exist. There is no possible world in which the very same individual, Socrates, exists but is a dog or a statue, say, instead of a genuine human being.

Individual essentialism (as I shall understand it) is the doctrine that individual objects have some of their (nontrivial) properties essentially. There are several questions asked about individual essentialism in prescriptive metaphysics. First, is the doctrine correct? Should we agree that individual things have essences, i.e., collections of (nontrivial) essential properties? Second, if individual essentialism is correct, which types of properties are the essential ones? Notice that certain candidates for essential properties may be natural kinds, like being human, while others may not be natural kinds at all. Third, what is the ontological status of individual essences? For example, if we consider a particular property as being essential to an individual thing, is this a mere projection or reflection of certain unity-imposing dispositions of our cognitive system, or is it a "mind-independent" fact about that thing?

A well-known defense of individual essentialism has been given by Kripke (1972). He suggests that one kind of property essential to an object is its *origin*. For example, Kripke asks, could Queen Elizabeth II have had a different origin than she actually had? Could she have been the child of President and Mrs. Truman? Well, we can certainly imagine a situation in which Mr. and Mrs. Truman had a child resembling her in many properties. Perhaps in some possible world Mr. and Mrs. Truman even had a child who actually became the Queen of England and was passed off as the child of other parents. But, says Kripke, this would still not be a situation in which Queen Elizabeth, *this very woman,* was the child of Mr. and Mrs. Truman. Instead, it would be a situation in which there was some other woman who had many of the properties that are in fact true of Elizabeth. Thus, Kripke concludes that it is an essential property of Elizabeth that she was born to her actual parents.

Notice the close similarity between this issue and the issue of identity through space or time. In the Ship of Theseus case, we asked which of the later ships, S_2 or S_3, was identical with the original ship, S_1. That is a question about cross-temporal identity. Here we are asking about identity across possible worlds. Is the Elizabeth of the actual world identical with the Elizabeth of a world in which she is the daughter of Harry and Bess Truman? This is a problem of trans-world identity ("trans-world heir lines," as one wit has dubbed it).

In both cases the evidence on which the conclusion is based stems entirely from people's intuitive reactions to various hypothetical situations: whether we would intuitively identify S_2 or S_3 with S_1, and whether we would intuitively identify the actual Elizabeth with the Elizabeth of the imagined world. Collecting intuitive reactions to many such cases, we then formulate general principles to cover them. On the basis of those principles we might say, for example, that ship S_3 is not identical with S_1 and that the daughter of the Trumans in the imagined world is not identical with Elizabeth of the actual world. Proceeding in this fashion, we might conclude with Kripke that Elizabeth II could not have been born of different parents, and hence that her origin is indeed an essential property of hers.

What is the ontological status, however, of this fact of individual essence? Is it a mind-independent fact, or is it merely a reflection of a cognitive (i.e., psychological) disposition to organize, segment, or parse the world's entities in certain ways? Most philosophers writing on this subject seem to assume that the matters in question are matters of mind-independent fact, not psychological disposition, thus taking an objectivist or realist interpretation of essentialism. But there is also a possible subjectivist or semi-subjectivist interpretation that would view essentialism as nothing but a fact or expression of human psychology. Determining which interpretation is correct is one of the issues of prescriptive metaphysics to which cognitive science can make some contributions.

Cognitive scientists (like Spelke) who study object unity (or identity) do so from the vantage point of psychological dispositions. The existence of psychological dispositions does not prove, though, that there aren't any mind-independent facts of the sort in question. Perhaps people's psychological dispositions are responsive to genuine mind-independent facts or can detect such facts. This difficult issue cannot be settled in a straightforward experimental fashion. However, perspectives gained by cognitive science in analogous domains can contribute to a sober assessment of the rival theories.

We have already seen in the case of color that hue categorizations are to a substantial degree the artifacts of our (highly contingent) color-coding system. The existence and position of unique hues, for example, is very much a function of the particulars of the opponent-processing system. Although we *seem* to detect an extra-mental fact about a color when we see a pure green or pure yellow, in an important sense the "purity" we experience is merely an artifact of our neural processing system. Similarly, when we intuit that the imagined child of Mr. and Mrs. Truman is not (the actual world's) Queen

Elizabeth, it may again seem that we are in touch with an extra-mental fact. But the only relevant facts of the matter may be the cognitive mechanisms that govern our cross-world unifying practices.

How exactly might cognitive science contribute to this conclusion? It may be in a position (eventually, if not now) to assure us that there is a cognitivist story to be told that explains the existence of our intuitive reactions and their interpersonal uniformity without appeal to any "detection" of extra-mental modal facts. We might then be in the situation of those who reject the inference from religious experience to theism on the ground that the religious experience can be explained purely psychologically, without reference to divine sources. If cognitive science can explain the occurrence of cross-world identity intuitions in purely psychological terms, without positing or implying exposure to corresponding modal facts, this would undercut the putative evidence for an objectivist or realist type of individual essentialism.

Cognitive science can also be relevant to the problem of whether principles of unity stem from conventions of language or from extra-linguistic cognitive structures. We saw earlier how Spelke's experiments on infants revealed highly determinate principles of unity at work prior to language acquisition. This finding clearly eliminates language as the sole source of unitizing, at least in the case of spatial and temporal unity. Whether similar evidence can be found for modal unity (unity across possible worlds) remains to be seen. In any case, there is certainly a role for cognitive science in locating the source(s) of unity intuitions and in helping to pinpoint the proper ontological status of facts about unity (or identity). In so doing, cognitive science would contribute to prescriptive metaphysics.

Cognitive science has a great deal to say that should be of interest to metaphysics. We have illustrated this dialogue by reference to object unity, categorial schemes, color, and essence. But other problems of metaphysics, such as the nature of causality, may also be open to helpful contributions from cognitive science.

Suggestions for Further Reading

For elaboration of the conceptions of descriptive and prescriptive metaphysics, see chapters 2 and 3 of Goldman (1992a), entitled "Metaphysics, Mind, and Mental Science" and "Cognition and Modal Metaphysics." The second of these chapters also has a more detailed discussion of individual essentialism and cognitive science.

A good philosophical study of unity principles is Hirsch (1982). Psychological perspectives are found in Jackendoff (1983), chapters 3 and 8, and Spelke (1990a) [R].

Examples of concept generation by analogical extension are found in Lakoff and Johnson (1980), Lakoff (1987), Jackendoff (1987) [R], and Talmy (1988).

Classic philosophical works on language and ontological commitment are Quine (1960, 1973). Recent discussions of related topics in the cognitivist literature are: Soja, Carey, and Spelke (1991) [R], Macnamara (1986), and Markman (1989).

The literature on color, both in philosophy and cognitive science, is massive. Three recent works that address both the metaphysical and the scientific dimensions are Hardin (1988) [R], Hilbert (1987), and Thompson, Palacios, and Varela (1992).

The revival of essentialism is heavily due to Kripke (1972) and Putnam (1975). Developmental psychologists who see scientific essentialist leanings in children include Carey (1985), Keil (1989), and Gelman and Wellman (1991).

Chapter Five

Ethics

Three Roles for Cognitive Science

The final branch of philosophy to be examined in this book is moral theory. There are three groups of questions relevant to moral theory that cognitive science might hope to answer. The first of these concerns the cognitive materials deployed by moral judges or evaluators in thinking about moral matters. The language of morals includes words like *good, right, just, fair, honest,* and so forth. What do users of these words mentally associate with them? How are the concepts of justice and fairness represented? And are such representations wholly determined by the cultural environment, or are there perhaps innate structures that dispose cognizers toward certain conceptions of fairness, just distribution, and so forth?

The second group of questions concerns hedonic states, which play a particularly crucial role in moral theory. A wide range of moral theories invoke such notions as *happiness, well-being, utility,* or *welfare* as critical determinants of the rightness or justice of actions and social policies. What can cognitive science tell us about the nature and determinants of these states? To what extent, for example, is your happiness affected by comparing your own condition with that of others or by comparing your present with your past condition? Answers to these questions have a bearing on the extent to which economic prosperity or other substantive endowments determine levels of happiness.

Our third set of questions concerns the motivational properties of human agents and the way they should be considered in appraising moral theories. Many ethical principles call for some degree, often a high degree, of altruism, and many theorists wonder whether such altruism is compatible with people's motivational structure. Just how egoistic are human beings? What mental capacities do they have, if any, that promote altruism, and how robust are these capacities? These questions must be addressed by empirical psychology.

The Mental Structure of Moral Cognition

In discussing the nature of moral cognition we set aside ontological issues about morality—whether there are such things as moral "facts"—as well as epistemological questions of whether we have perceptual or intuitive access to such facts. We restrict ourselves to the way that ordinary people *think* about moral attributes, regardless of whether such thought "corresponds" or "answers to" some sort of independent reality.

It used to be assumed in many areas of philosophy that words were susceptible to strict definitions that specified *individually necessary and jointly sufficient conditions* for the application of the word. Stephen Stich (forthcoming) points out that this kind of assumption seems to have been made by Plato in his treatment of moral terms. In the dialogue *Euthyphro* we find the following passage concerning piety.

> *Socrates.* And what is piety, and what is impiety? ... Tell me what is the nature of this idea, and then I shall have a standard to which I may look, and by which I may measure actions, whether yours or those of any one else, and then I shall be able to say that such and such an action is pious, such another impious.

> *Euthyphro.* I will tell you, if you like. ... Piety ... is that which is dear to the gods, and impiety is that which is not dear to them.
>
> *Socrates.* Very good Euthyphro, you have now given me the sort of answer which I wanted. But whether what you say is true or not I cannot as yet tell (Plato 1937, 386–387).

According to Euthyphro, being dear to the gods is a *necessary condition* for being pious and a *sufficient condition* as well.

This general approach to concepts—the approach that expects to find necessary and sufficient conditions—is called in cognitive science the *classical view.* This old and influential approach, however, has recently run into tough sledding. True, some concepts seem to conform to the classical view: *grandmother* seems to be definable as someone who is female and is the parent of a parent. But the collective work of psychologists, linguists, and philosophers has recently challenged the applicability of this view to many other concepts, especially *natural-kind* concepts like *dog, daisy, fruit,* or *bird* (see Smith 1990).

One experimental finding is that people can reliably order the instances of natural-kind concepts with respect to how "typical" or "representative" they are of the concept. For the concept *fruit,* for example, apples and peaches are considered typical, raisins and figs less typical, and pumpkins and olives atypical. These ratings correlate with performance in a wide variety of tasks. If subjects are asked to decide as quickly as possible if an item is an instance of a concept (for example, "Is a fig a fruit?"), they are faster the more typical the instance. Another task is memory retrieval. If asked to generate from memory all instances of a concept, subjects retrieve typical before atypical instances.

These typicality effects seem inhospitable to the classical view. They suggest that not all instances of a natural-kind concept are equal; yet equality is what one might expect if every instance met the same definition of the necessary-and-sufficient-conditions type. The argument against the classical view is strengthened by the additional finding that virtually all the properties listed by subjects as relevant to a concept are not strictly necessary, e.g., the property of being sweet for *fruit* or the properties of flying and singing for *bird.* (Penguins don't fly and vultures don't sing.) Similar findings apply to other concepts, including artifact concepts such as *furniture* or *clothing.*

The typicality findings have led to a modification of the classical view of concepts: Concepts are represented in terms of properties that need not be strictly necessary but are frequently present in instances of the concept. These properties are weighted by their frequency or by their perceptual salience. A collection of such properties is called a *prototype.* Under the prototype view, an object is categorized as an instance of a concept if it is sufficiently similar to the prototype, similarity being determined (in part) by the number of properties in the prototype possessed by the instance and by the sum of their weights. This view can explain many of the typicality findings. For example, typical instances are categorized faster than atypical instances because categorization involves determining that an item exceeds some critical level of similarity to the prototype, and the more similar the item is to the prototype, the faster this determination can be made (see Smith 1990; Smith and Medin 1981).

How does concept representation bear on moral philosophy? It turns out that in many areas of moral philosophy there is much controversy over whether a certain item is an instance of a certain concept. For example, on the issue of abortion it is controversial whether a fetus is an instance of a *person* (or a *human life*). Often people try to settle this issue by trying to find necessary and sufficient conditions for being a person. This search presupposes, however, that such a definition is in principle forthcoming, that we (tacitly) represent the concept of a person in terms of necessary and sufficient conditions. It may be, however, that our representation of this concept, like many other concepts, has a prototype structure. This might support a conclusion that the fetus is an instance of *person* but a highly atypical instance. No such conclusion could directly settle the abortion controversy, of course, but it could significantly affect our theoretical reflections on the issue.

A proper understanding of concepts and conceptualization may be even more important to moral philosophy by serving to forestall hasty conclusions. Some moral philosophers (e.g., Ayer 1936), seeing that it is difficult to give "classical" or "reductive" definitions of moral terms, have concluded that descriptivism in ethics should be replaced by emotivism. In other words, they have concluded that moral words do not have descriptive meaning but only express feelings or give commands ("do this," "don't do that," etc.). But once we appreciate that very few words have classical or reductive definitions, we can see that it is a mistake to infer from the absence of such definitions that moral words lack descriptive content. (This point was suggested by Holly Smith, personal communication.)

Another proposal for dealing with the typicality results hypothesizes that concepts are (sometimes) represented by one or more specific exemplars, or instances, that the cognizer has encountered. Thus I might represent *dog* by the set of dogs I have encountered or by some specific dogs encountered when I first learned the term. On this *exemplar view,* categorization occurs by activating the mental representations of one or more exemplars of the concept and then assessing the similarity between the exemplars and the item to be categorized (see Medin and Schaffer 1978; Estes 1986).

The exemplar theory is particularly intriguing from the standpoint of moral theory, as Stich (forthcoming) points out. Moral theorists often assume that people's usage of moral terms is underpinned by some set of *rules* or *principles* they learn to associate with those terms—rules governing *honesty,* for example, or *fairness.* The exemplar theory suggests, however, that what moral learning consists in may not be (primarily) the learning of rules but the acquisition of pertinent *exemplars* or *examples.* This notion would accord with the observable fact that people, especially children, have an easier time assimilating the import of parables, myths, and fables than abstract principles. A morally suitable *role model* may be didactically more effective than a set of behavioral maxims. If this theory is correct, it is an important lesson for moral philosophy, which often tries to reconstruct the nature of ordinary moral judgment. Ordinary moral thinking may consist more in comparing contemplated actions with stored exemplars of good and bad behavior than with the formulation and deduction of consequences from abstract principles. Of course, the moral theorist may choose to spurn common patterns of moral thought, to try to replace them with something preferable. Before such a revisionary move is considered, however, we may want to have the facts straight about how "folk morality" proceeds.

Innate Constraints on Moral Thinking

Let us return now to the widely held view that moral thought somehow includes material of a rule-like nature. The method of uncovering the system of rules underlying intuitive moral judgments may then be compared, as John Rawls (1971) has done, to methods of modern linguistics. Following Noam Chomsky, linguists typically assume that speakers of a natural language have internalized a system of generative grammatical rules that play a central role in language production and comprehension as well as in the production of "intuitions" by speakers about the grammaticality of sentences presented to them. In attempting to discover what speakers have internalized, linguists construct systems of generative rules and check them against speakers' intuitions.

Stich points to a further possible analogy between grammatical and moral theory. Chomsky has long maintained that grammatical rules are so complex that a child could not learn them from the limited data available to him if he were using "unbiased," general-purpose learning algorithms. The stimuli are too "impoverished," according to Chomsky, to permit this possibility. Instead, he says, there must be innate constraints on learning that guide the acquisition of grammars. Such constraints would imply that the range of grammars a child could actually learn is a small and highly structured subset of the set of logically possible grammars. All the grammars of actual languages, of course, fall within this subset. An intriguing possible analogy is that there may be innate constraints on moral thinking that similarly restrict the range of "humanly possible" moral systems to a relatively small subset of the logically possible systems.

One popular candidate for an innate moral constraint is a predisposition against *incest.* Most cultures have taboos against sexual intercourse among close relatives, and even when taboos are lacking, incest is typically infrequent. The low rate of incest is often said to result from a genetic propensity to refrain from sexual relations with those with whom one has been reared. The thesis appears to have some empirical support, though it encounters difficulties when examined in detail (see van den Berghe 1983; Kitcher 1985).

The case of incest involves a putatively innate predisposition concerning a specific type of act. Constraints on moral thinking, however, may have a more abstract structure. Precisely this idea has been suggested by Alan Fiske (in press, 1991). On the basis of a wide survey of anthropological, sociological, and psychological findings, Fiske postulates the existence of four elementary forms of sociality that serve as people's models in constructing "approved" styles of social interaction and social structure: (1) Communal Sharing, (2) Authority Ranking, (3) Equality Matching, and (4) Market

Pricing. Because these same four structures seem to be universal, i.e., found to some extent in all cultures, and since they emerge in all the major domains of social life, Fiske suggests as a plausible inference that they are rooted in structures of the human mind.

To get a sense of Fiske's theory, let us look at the four models in a little detail. Under Communal Sharing (CS), relationships are based on the idea that all group members are equivalent and undifferentiated. Given a criterion for group membership, possessions of the group are then conferred on all group members equally, whatever their individual contributions may be. For example, in many hunting and gathering societies, people share the meat of game animals across the whole band: The hunter who killed the animal may get less than many others, and people give food, tools, and utensils to anyone who asks for them. In most societies this kind of sharing of material things is common among close kin and sometimes among other associates. At a commensal meal, no one keeps track of who eats how much. Other manifestations of the CS structure are holding land in commons and organizing production so that people work collectively without assessing individual inputs or assigning distinct responsibilities. The role of material things in Authority Ranking (AR) relationships is quite different. When people transfer things from person to person in an AR mode, higher-ranking people get more and better things—and get them sooner—than their subordinates. Higher-ranking people may preempt rare or valuable items so that inferior people get none at all. Subjects may have to pay goods in tribute to rulers, or authorities may simply appropriate what they want. Conversely, a principle of noblesse oblige usually obtains in AR relations, so that authorities have an obligation to be generous and to exercise pastoral responsibility to protect and sustain their subordinates. Fiske interprets much of religion as a manifestation of the AR model. He sees the prominence of AR in many religions as evidence that humans have a proclivity for projecting this schema onto the world as a way of interpreting, judging, and validating experience.

Social scientists have tended to treat hierarchical relationships as if they were ultimately based on pure force or coercive power. Fiske instead postulates a psychological receptivity toward establishing authority relationships. He points out that AR, like CS, emerges in a great variety of domains of social action, thought, and evaluation. Linear orderings are prominent in exchange, distribution, the organization of work, the meaning of land, and so forth. The congruence of structure across such diverse contexts and cultures suggests that the structure is the product of the one thing that is constant across them all—the human mind.

The third elementary form of relationship, Equality Matching (EM), or sometimes called *balanced reciprocity,* is an egalitarian, one-for-one exchange, exemplified in our culture by the exchange of Christmas gifts. For the purpose of such interchanges, people ignore the differentiating qualities that might make one object more desirable or valuable than another. Similarly, a dinner party matches a dinner party—within a range of possibilities that the culture defines rather precisely. In order to count and match in such cases, equivalence classes have to be defined. Once they are, however, categorical equivalence permits relationships to be balanced despite differences that actually exist between the entities exchanged. Anthropologists have pointed out that balanced reciprocity is often used as a way of establishing relationships between strangers or reestablishing amicable relations among former enemies.

Market Pricing (MP) relationships are based on a model of proportionality in social relations in which ratios and rates become the important factors. People in an MP relationship usually reduce all the relevant features and components under consideration to a single value or utility metric which allows the comparison of many qualitatively and quantitatively diverse factors. This model is extremely prevalent, of course, in our own society and perhaps needs no further elaboration.

Fiske emphasizes that his four hypothesized models are just elementary models which are rarely used alone. Two friends may share tapes and records freely with each other (CS), work on a task at which one is an expert and imperiously directs the other (AR), divide equally the cost of gas on a trip (EM), and transfer a bicycle from one to the other for a market-value price (MP). He also emphasizes that culture is decisive in selecting which models are to be implemented in which relationships and in fixing relevant parameters. But the basic models themselves, he postulates, have a psychological origin. It is much too early to decide whether this large-scale theory can be substantiated because many difficult questions obviously arise. However, it at least provides an illustration of the way in which psychological constraints may help fix extant systems of morality.

Judgments of Subjective Well-Being

Let us now shift gears and turn to our second set of questions that bear on moral theory—questions that concern hedonic states. Most modern moral theories, especially those in the utilitarian tradition, assign an important place to the concepts of happiness, utility, welfare, or well-being. Morally good actions or social policies are widely thought to be ones that promote the general welfare, or encourage an appropriate distribution of welfare. The exact nature of happiness, welfare, or well-being, however, needs detailed investigation, and this is a topic to which cognitive psychology is making interesting contributions.

While it is often assumed that wealth and other external conditions of life promote happiness or satisfaction, it is unclear a priori just how strong a correlation there is. We therefore need better measures of well-being. To this end, social science researchers have devised survey techniques in which respondents are asked to report how happy and satisfied they are with their life as a whole and with various life domains. These so-called *subjective social indicators* are used as measures of subjective well-being. As Angus Campbell (1981, 23) points out, the "use of these measures is based on the assumption that all the countless experiences people go through from day to day add to . . . global feelings of well-being, that these feelings remain relatively constant over extended periods, and that people can describe them with candor and accuracy." These assumptions, however, have proved problematic. The relationship between individuals' objective life conditions and their subjective sense of well-being was found to be weak and sometimes counterintuitive. Poor people are sometimes happier than rich ones; patients three years after a cancer operation were found to be happier than a healthy control group; and paralyzed accident victims were happier with their lives than one might expect. Moreover, measures of well-being have been shown to have a low test-retest reliability (consistency), usually hovering around .40, and these measures were found to be quite sensitive to influence from preceding questions in a questionnaire or interview.

Cognitive social psychologists seek to understand these findings. From their perspective, reports about happiness and satisfaction with one's life are not necessarily valid readouts of an internal state of personal well-being. Rather, they are constructions to a particular question posed at a particular time and subject to a variety of transient influences. Norbert Schwarz and Fritz Strack (1991) report their own and other psychologists' research into the question of how people go about trying to answer the survey queries.

Suppose you are a respondent asked the question: "Taking all things together, how would you say things are these days?

Would you say you are very happy, pretty happy, or not too happy?" Unfortunately, "taking all things together" is a difficult mental task. Indeed, in instructing the respondent to think about all aspects of his or her life, it requests something impossible. Thus, say Schwarz and Strack, you are unlikely to retrieve all information that potentially bears on this judgment but instead will probably truncate the search process as soon as enough information comes to mind that you can form the judgment with a reasonable degree of subjective certainty. Thus, the judgment reflects the implications of the information that comes to mind most easily.

How is this accessible information used? It has been found that such use depends heavily on the standard of comparison that is momentarily established, which can be a function of salient information about one's own previous experiences or about other people and their experiences. In an experiment by Strack, Schwarz, and Gschneidinger (1985), subjects in one group were instructed to recall and write down a very negative event in their lives, while subjects in another group were instructed to recall and write down a very positive event in their lives. Within each group, half of the subjects were asked to recall a recent event and half were asked to recall a past event. Subjects were then asked to rate their well-being on a 10-point scale. This procedure yields a 2 x 2 design in which the recalled event was either positive or negative, recent or in the past. For the recent events, the results were hardly surprising. Recalling a positive recent event made people feel good, whereas thinking about a negative recent event made people feel less happy. The results for past events were more surprising: Ratings of well-being were higher for those who recalled a past negative event than for those who recalled a past positive event. It thus appears that the effect of comparison to one's past is quite substantial. Similar effects have been observed by Strack, Schwarz, and colleagues concerning comparisons with others (see Schwarz and Strack 1991). Subjects evaluated their own life more favorably when they met a handicapped experimental confederate, or listened to such a confederate describe how a severe medical condition interfered with his enjoyment of life. The impact of the confederate's description was even more pronounced when the seating arrangements rendered the confederate visible while the subject was actually filling out the happiness report. Such findings emphasize the role of temporary accessibility in the choice of comparison standards.

Endowment and Contrast in Judgments of Well-Being

Building partly on the work of Schwarz and Strack, Amos Tversky and Dale Griffin (1991) have constructed a model of hedonic judgments using the notions of *endowment* and *contrast.* The endowment effect of an event represents its direct contribution to one's happiness or satisfaction. Events also exercise an indirect contrast effect on the evaluation of subsequent events. A positive experience makes us happy, but also renders similar experiences less exciting. A negative experience makes us unhappy but helps us appreciate subsequent experiences that are less bad. Thus, the hedonic impact of an event reflects a balance of its endowment and contrast effects. A simple example illustrates the point. A professor from a small midwestern town attends a conference in New York and enjoys dinner at an outstanding French restaurant. This event contributes to her endowment, but it also gives rise to a contrast effect. A later meal in the local French restaurant becomes somewhat less satisfying by comparison with the great meal in New York.

Tversky and Griffin use their endowment-contrast model to explain some of the findings reported in Strack, Schwarz, and Gschneidinger 1985. Recall that these findings included the following "reversal": Ratings of well-being were higher for subjects who recalled a past negative event than for those who recalled a past positive event. The endowment-contrast scheme explains this as follows. For recent events there is no room for contrast; hence we get a positive endowment effect for the positive event and a negative endowment effect for the negative event. The recall of past events, however, introduces a contrast with the present: People feel positive about the present when recalling past negative events and negative about the present when recalling past positive ones. Because recent events are more salient than past events, the endowment effect is greater for recent events than for past events. For past events, the contrast component offsets the endowment component and produces the observed reversal.

Students of well-being focus on *judgments* of satisfaction or happiness. Another paradigm for the study of welfare, dominant in economics, focuses on *choice* rather than judgment. In this paradigm, a person is said to be better off in State A than in State B if he or she chooses State A over State B. In addition, the concept of *utility* has been used in economics and decision theory in two different senses: (1) *experience value,* the degree of satisfaction associated with the actual experience of an outcome, and (2) *decision value,* the choiceworthiness of an anticipated outcome. Tversky and Griffin, having drawn this distinction, point out that in many situations experience values, as expressed in self-ratings, diverge from decision values, as inferred from choice. One obvious point of divergence is that we often choose options that do not actually make us happy; things just do not turn out as we expect them to. However, even if judgments of well-being are restricted to *anticipated* satisfaction, choices and judgments of prospective well-being can produce discrepancies. When people are asked to assess the hedonic value of some future states (e.g., employment situations) they try to imagine what it would feel like to experience those states. But when asked to choose among these states, they tend to search for reasons or arguments to justify their choice. And the resultant assessments may well differ.

To illustrate this choice-judgment discrepancy, Tversky and Griffin gave the following information to subjects:

> Imagine that you have just completed a graduate degree in Communications and you are considering one-year jobs at two different magazines.
>
> (A) At Magazine A, you are offered a job paying $35,000. However, the other workers who have the same training and experience as you do are making $38,000.
> (B) At Magazine B, you are offered a job paying $33,000. However, the other workers who have the same training and experience as you do are making $30,000 (Tversky and Griffin 1991, 114).

Approximately half the subjects were asked "Which job would you choose to take?" while the other half were asked, "At which job would you be happier?" The results confirmed the prediction that the salary would dominate the choice whereas the comparison with others would loom larger in judgment. Eighty-four percent of the subjects given the choice question preferred the job with the higher absolute salary and lower relative position, while 62 percent of the subjects given the happiness-prediction question anticipated higher satisfaction in the job with the lower absolute salary but higher relative position.

The choice-judgment discrepancy raises an intriguing question: Which is the correct or more appropriate measure of well-being? Tversky and Griffin suggest that both choice and judgment provide relevant data for the assessment of well-being but that neither one is entirely satisfactory. Notice that the judgment criterion, however, raises doubts about the most basic principle of welfare economics—Pareto optimality. Pareto optimality says that an allocation of resources is acceptable if it improves everybody's lot. Viewed as a choice criterion, this principle is irresistible. It is hard to object to a policy that improves your lot just because it improves the lot of someone else even more. But Tversky and Griffin point out that this choice focuses exclusively on endowment and neglects contrast altogether. Contrast effects can create widespread unhappiness. Consider a policy that doubles the salary of a few people in an organization and increases all other salaries by 5 percent. Even though all salaries rise (conforming with Pareto optimality), it is doubtful that this change will make most people happy. There is a great deal of evidence (e.g., Brickman 1975; Brickman and Campbell 1971) that people's reported satisfaction does not depend just on their objective situation but also depends largely on their relative position. Surveys indicate that wealthier people are slightly happier than people with less money, but substantial increases in everyone's income and standard of living do not raise the reported level of happiness (Easterlin 1974).

It seems clear that any substantive moral or social theory at all concerned with happiness, welfare, or satisfaction should take these findings and analyses into account. This is a vivid illustration of how cognitive psychology bears on moral theory.

Empathy

Let us turn now to the third group of questions about moral theory, those concerning the possible psychological mechanisms that might promote altruistic behavior. A lot has been written in the philosophical literature on the exact definition of "altruism," but a precise definition need not concern us here. Instead I shall turn directly to a plausible hypothesis about one psychological mechanism that might promote altruism: the process of *empathy.* The phenomenon of empathy has been characterized in a number of closely related but different ways. Here I shall link it directly to the simulation process sketched at the end of Chapter 3.

The simulation process consists first of taking the perspective of another person, i.e., imaginatively assuming one or more of the other person's mental states. Such perspective taking might be instigated by observing that person's situation and behavior or by simply being told about them, as when one reads a history book or a novel. Psychological processes then (automatically) operate on the initial "pretend" states to generate further states that (in favorable cases) are similar to, or homologous to, the target person's states. I conceive of empathy as a special case of the simulation process in which the output states are *affective* or *emotional* states rather than purely cognitive or conative states like believing or desiring. Furthermore, just as the simulator is generally aware of his states as simulations of the target agent's states, so the empathizer is assumed to be aware of his vicarious affects and emotions as representatives of the emotions or affects of the target agent. Thus, empathy consists of a sort of "mimicking" of one person's affective state by that of another. (More precisely, this is *veridical* empathy; mistaken empathy is also possible, though I shall neglect it henceforth.) This characterization accords with at least some of the definitions in the psychological literature. Mark Barnett (1987), for example, defines empathy as "the vicarious experiencing of an emotion that is congruent with, but not necessarily identical to, the emotion of another individual."

While almost everyone experiences empathy at one time or another, it remains to be shown how fundamental and robust a phenomenon it is and whether the description given above is psychologically sustainable. Does it even make sense, for example, to construe empathic states as "similar," "congruent," or "homologous" to the genuine affective states of the target agent? What exactly are the respects of similarity or congruence?

At this point in time we cannot specify the precise respects of similarity between original and vicarious affective states. This is insufficient reason, however, to deny the existence of significant similarities. Neither can we specify precisely how visual imagery resembles actual visual perception. Nonetheless, there is ample demonstration of significant respects of similarity between the two domains (see Finke and Shepard 1986; Kosslyn 1980, 1990). If comparable experimental creativity were invested in the field of vicarious affect, it would not be surprising to find analogous points of similarity.

Meanwhile, there are plenty of experimental demonstrations of mimicking, "tracking," or resonating to the mental states of others that make such phenomena appear to be quite pervasive features of the human organism. Some of these may be primitive precursors of empathy rather than strict empathy of the type defined here. However, the fact that many of these phenomena develop very early in life also suggests the presence of an innate mechanism, or several such mechanisms.

One phenomenon of interest is *joint visual attention*, the propensity of infants to follow the gaze of another person. Butterworth and colleagues studied six-month-old babies and found that when the mother turns and visually inspects a target, her baby will look to the same side of the room to which the mother is attending and will be quite accurate in locating the object referred to by the mother's change of gaze (Butterworth and Cochran 1980; Butterworth 1991). Here we have one early phenomenon of "tracking" or "mimicking" another person's mental orientation.

A second phenomenon, more pertinent to affect, is *emotional contagion*, familiar to all of us through the infectious effects of smiles and laughter. The primitive basis of emotional contagion has been experimentally studied in the reactive crying of newborns. Simner (1971) presented two- to four-day-old infants with tapes of various auditory stimuli, including (1) spontaneous crying by a five-day-old neonate, (2) spontaneous crying by an infant who was five and a half months old, (3) a computer-synthesized replication of a newborn cry, (4) the baby's own spontaneous crying (previously recorded), and (5) white noise that was equivalent to crying in sound intensity. Simner found that the sound of neonatal crying (1 and 4) produced significantly more reactive crying in these newborns than did either white noise, the older infant's cry, or the synthetic cry.

Another example of resonant emotion occurs in the context of *social referencing.* Klinnert (1981) presented twelve- and eighteen-month-old infants with novel and somewhat forbidding toys in a laboratory playroom in their mothers' presence. Mothers were instructed to pose facial expressions conveying either fear, joy, or neutral emotion. For those infants who regularly referenced the mother, i.e., looked at her to "check" on her attitude, maternal facial expressions had a profound effect. When the mothers were smiling, the infants were significantly more likely to move away from them to approach the toy than when the mothers were not smiling, but when the mothers displayed fear, the infants were more likely to retreat. Additional evidence showed that such behavior was mediated through the arousal of a resonant emotion in the children, who themselves showed negative affect in response to the mothers' negative affect.

The foregoing cases of emotional contagion are not clear cases of empathy because they may not involve the stage of perspective taking. However, other experimental work shows that congruent emotion may plausibly be produced by means of perspective taking. First, Berger (1962) had subjects observe a target person performing a task. He led them to believe that the target was either receiving electric shock or not, after which the target person either jerked his or her arm or did not. All observers were told that they themselves would not be shocked during the study. Berger reasoned that both a painful stimulus in the environment (shock) and a distress response (movement) would lead observers to infer that the target person was experiencing pain. Berger found that observers informed of both shock and movement were themselves more physiologically aroused than observers in the other three conditions. Although Berger's manipulations did not directly address perspective taking, it is plausible to suppose that the observers did indeed engage in perspective taking.

The results of Ezra Stotland (1969), previously reported in Chapter 3, explicitly addressed imaginative projection. All of Stotland's subjects watched someone else whose hand was strapped into a machine. The subjects were told that this machine generated painful heat. Some were instructed just to watch the man carefully, some to imagine the way he was feeling, and some to imagine themselves in his place. Using both physiological and verbal measures of empathy, the experimental results clearly showed that the deliberate acts of imagination produced a greater response than just watching.

It is noteworthy that these results are not restricted to painful or distressing experiences. In the study reported by Stotland, subjects who witnessed another person experiencing what they perceived to be pleasure reported, relative to controls, that they found participating in the study to be a pleasant experience. Similarly, Dennis Krebs (1975) found that participants reported feeling relatively bad when watching someone whom they thought was about to receive an electric shock and relatively good when watching someone about to receive a reward.

An insightful observation of "positive" empathy is presented by Adam Smith, whose book *The Theory of Moral Sentiments* contains some of the most brilliant discussions of empathy (which he called "sympathy").

> When we have read a book or poem so often that we can no longer find any amusement in reading it by ourselves, we can still take pleasure in reading it to a companion. To him it has all

> the graces of novelty; we enter into the surprise and admiration which it naturally excites in him, but which it is no longer capable of exciting in us; we consider all the ideas which it presents rather in the light in which they appear to him, than in that in which they appear to ourselves, and we are amused by sympathy with his amusement which thus enlivens our own (Smith 1759/1976, 14).

Granted that the mental mimicking or "resonating" to others *occasionally* occurs, how robust and prevalent a phenomenon is it? Some evidence in this regard may come from the prevalence of *motor* mimicry, a highly robust phenomenon. Observation of motor mimicry is at least two centuries old and has recently been demonstrated experimentally (see Bavelas et al. 1987 for a review). Adam Smith described it as follows: "When we see a stroke aimed, and just ready to fall upon the leg or arm of another person, we naturally shrink and draw back on our leg or our own arm" (1759/1976, 10). Numerous other writers have commented on the same phenomenon, including Spencer (1870), Darwin (1872), McDougall (1908), Allport (1968), and Mead (1934). (Mead was a great champion of the "role-taking" idea.)

Clark Hull (1933) first brought motor mimicry into the experimental laboratory through a method that could be recorded. He arranged for an observer to see another person straining and reaching, and by surreptitiously pinning a string to the observer's clothing and attaching this string to a rotary event recorder, Hull obtained a trace of the mimetic movements. O'Toole and Dubin (1968), followers of Mead, conducted two full-scale investigations. In one, observers swayed forward while an actor strained to reach forward, and in the second, mothers opened their own mouths while spoon-feeding their infants (the mother most often opened her own mouth *after* the baby had, evidence of true mimicking rather than just trying to induce the infant to imitate). Additional experiments further demonstrate the ubiquity of the phenomenon.

A natural way to explain motor mimicry is in terms of *mental* mimicry: People mentally take the role of another and fail to inhibit (to take "off line") the behavioral upshot of this mental role taking. If correct, this hypothesis suggests an extensive prominence for role taking in our mental lives. (Bavelas et al. 1987 offer a slightly different hypothesis, but it does not seem to me to be a genuine rival to the role-taking one.) True, motor mimicry is often not accompanied by phenomenological awareness of perspective taking (nor accompanied by awareness of the mimetic behavior itself). But it is entirely consonant with cognitive science to postulate the tacit occurrence of the relevant mental processes. Assuming, then, that mental mimicking of others is a prevalent phenomenon and that it offers wide opportunity for affective resonance, empathic feelings may well be quite widespread, not a rare or merely occasional occurrence.

Empathy and Descriptive Ethics

Let us assume, then, that empathy is a genuine and fairly pervasive facet of human life. What are the consequences for moral theory? And what relevance can further empirical investigation of empathy have to moral theory? Let me first divide moral or ethical theory into two components: *descriptive* and *prescriptive* ethics. (This distinction is analogous to the distinction drawn in Chapter 4 between descriptive and prescriptive metaphysics.) Descriptive ethics in turn has two branches. The first branch seeks to describe and explain the acceptance of the various moral codes in different cultures and subcultures while the second seeks to describe and explain the extent of people's *conformity* with the codes to which they subscribe. This second branch focuses heavily on motivational factors. What enables an agent to act on her moral creed or inhibits her from doing so? Prescriptive ethics would, of course, be concerned with the formulation and justification of a "proper" or "correct" moral system. But this sector of ethics must also be concerned with motivational factors, for reasons to be explained.

The empirical study of empathy is relevant to all of these branches and subbranches of ethics. Historically, a key role for empathy in descriptive ethics was championed by Arthur Schopenhauer. The primary ethical phenomenon, according to Schopenhauer, is compassion, which he characterized as the vicarious "participation" in the suffering of another.

> How is it possible for *another's* weal and woe to move my will immediately ... ? [H]ow is it possible for *another's* weal and woe to become directly my motive ... ? Obviously only through that other man's becoming the *ultimate object* of my will in the same way as I myself otherwise am, and hence through my directly desiring *his* weal and not *his* woe just as immediately as I ordinarily do only *my own.* But this necessarily presupposes that, in the case of his *woe* as such, I suffer directly with him, I feel *his* woe just as I ordinarily feel my own; and, likewise, I directly desire his weal in the same way I otherwise desire only my own. But this requires that I am in some way *identified with him.* ... Now since I do not exist *inside the other man's skin,* then only by means of the *knowledge* I have of him, that is, of the representation of him in my head, can I identify myself with him to such an extent that my deed declares that difference abolished. However, the process here analyzed is not one that is imagined or invented; on the contrary it is perfectly real and indeed by no means infrequent. It is the everyday phenomenon of *compassion,* of the immediate *participation,* independent of all ulterior considerations, primarily in the *suffering* of another. ... It is simply and solely this compassion that is the real basis of all *voluntary* justice and *genuine* loving-kindness (Schopenhauer 1841/1965, 143–144, italics in original).

Schopenhauer assigns compassion a critical place in explaining the cross-cultural display of moral behavior in human life.

> [T]he foundation of morals or the incentive to morality as laid down by me is the only one that can boast of a real, and extensive, effectiveness. ... [D]espite the great variety of religions in the world, the degree of morality, or rather immorality, shows absolutely no corresponding variety, but is essentially pretty much the same everywhere. ... [Unlike the ineffectiveness of religion] the moral incentive that is put forward by me [viz., compassion] ... displays a decided and truly wonderful effectiveness at all times, among all nations, in all the situations of life, even in a state of anarchy and amid the horrors of revolutions and wars (Schopenhauer 1841/1965, 170, 172).

Schopenhauer thus views compassion as the source of moral principles and the ultimate root of compliance with such principles.

The traditional task of descriptive ethics—identifying and explaining the moral systems found in various cultures—has taken a new focus in recent years as many writers have begun to point to differences in moral systems or orientations even within a single culture. In particular, they claim to find gender differences in moral orientation. Carol Gilligan (1982) is probably the most cited defender of such a hypothesis. The question of whether such differences exist, and if so what their source might be, is a good example of a subject ripe for empirical inquiry. Gilligan claims that women have a moral orientation that focuses on "caring" and "connecting" rather than abstract rights or justice. This thesis, however, has been criticized on empirical grounds. In a series of studies, Lawrence Walker (1984) and his colleagues found no statistically significant gender differences as measured within Lawrence Kohlberg's widely used moral stage framework. In a more recent study, Walker, DeVries, and Trevethan (1987) did find that females were more likely to choose personal over impersonal dilemmas as problems to talk about and to identify personal problems as the sort they confronted. Moreover, personal dilemmas were more likely to elicit a "care" response than a "justice" or "rights" response. Controlling for dilemma *content*, however, sex differences were still not found to be significant.

Gilligan's thesis, and similar theses advanced by other feminist writers, is particularly relevant to our discussion of descriptive ethics since a focus on caring and connecting might stem from more frequent or more salient empathy. Indeed, Gilligan quotes with approval Norma Haan's (1975) and Constance Holstein's (1976) research which indicates "that the moral judgments of women differ from those of men in the greater extent to which women's judgments are tied to feelings of empathy and compassion" (Gilligan 1982, 60). This debate over whether there is a psychological difference between the genders in the incidence or strength of empathy, which common sex stereotypes, of course, suggest, is a heavily researched topic, but the results are complex and inconclusive.

A principal complication in empathy research is the variety of measures used in its detection. Nancy Eisenberg and her colleague Randy Lennon (Eisenberg and Lennon 1983; Lennon and Eisenberg 1987) surveyed the results of experiments using the most popular methods of assessing empathy. In young children, this involves using picture/story stimuli and operationalizing empathy as the degree of match between self-report of emotion and the emotion appropriate to the protagonist in the vignette. In twenty-eight studies using this measure, most found no significant gender differences. In studies of school-age children and adults, the most widely used index is a self-report questionnaire. In sixteen studies of this sort females scored significantly higher than males. However, these differences may be due to biases in self-reports. Females are *expected* to be more concerned with others as well as more emotional than males, so both females and males may respond in ways consistent with sex-role stereotypes. Other measures of empathy include facial/gestural and vocal measures as well as physiological measures of empathy. Eisenberg and Lennon conclude that no significant gender differences are found on these measures.

Empathy and Prescriptive Ethics

Let us turn now to prescriptive ethics. Most writers would agree that a satisfactory prescriptive theory should be firmly rooted in human nature. It would be hard to defend any moral system as prescriptively valid that did not make important contact with human moral psychology. Much of ethical theory has focused on the human capacity for reason, a tradition most vividly exemplified by Kant. In recent literature, there is also a tendency to associate moral rationalism with highly *universalistic* moral norms and to associate emotionalism (as the contrasting approach might be dubbed) with a *particularist* point of view. Universalism requires the moral agent to consider everyone's pleasure or pain equally and impartially. It requires the agent to take up something like "the point of view of the universe." By contrast, particularism allows the agent to display some degree of partiality toward individuals with whom one has a personal affinity, such as family members, friends, students, or comrades. If we now consider the prospects of an empathy-based view of morality, it might seem natural for it to tilt toward particularism, as Lawrence Blum (1980, 1987), for example, suggests, because empathy inclines an agent toward actions that are responsive to those with whom he empathizes, and these are most likely to be people with whom personal contact is established.

However, it is not clear that an emphasis on empathy or sympathy necessarily dictates a particularist or "agent-centered" morality. A universalist may point out that empathy can be extended beyond personal contacts—for example, to characters in fiction or history. In fact, there have been sympathy-based theories, such as David Hume's, that are quite universalistic.

These issues can be viewed in a slightly different light if we consider the psychological constraints that might be imposed on a "correct" moral theory, i.e., a theory that can be considered correct *for human beings.* A moral code that is psychologically unrealizable by human beings, or just too demanding or difficult for people to satisfy, might be rejected as misguided or illegitimate. "Oughts" should not be imposed on people unless they are capable of fulfilling them. In other words, it is plausible to impose a constraint like Owen Flanagan's Principle of Minimal Psychological Realism: "Make sure when constructing a moral theory or projecting a moral ideal that the character, decision processing, and behavior prescribed are possible ... for creatures like us" (Flanagan 1991, 32). Moral theories like utilitarianism may fail to satisfy this principle because they may require more altruistic behavior, or more universalism, than is feasible for human beings. In its simplest form, utilitarianism says that a person should always choose actions that produce the greatest net happiness—where the happiness of everyone affected by an action is counted equally. If you are the agent, this means weighing other people's happiness as much as your own, the happiness of a neighbor's or a stranger's child as much as the happiness of your own child, and so forth. Some theorists worry that it is beyond the psychological capacity of human beings to comply with this precept. If so, Flanagan's constraint would require the rejection of utilitarianism as a moral theory.

This raises the question: Just what are people's capacities for altruism and for serving everyone's welfare equally as opposed to furthering their own welfare or that of specially related others. Here empathy again becomes particularly relevant, since it seems to be a prime mechanism in disposing us toward altruistic behavior. What exactly is the potential scope, extent, or power of empathy? Can we empathize with everyone equally? This problem worried Hume: "We sympathize more with persons contiguous to us, than with persons remote from us: With our acquaintances, than with strangers; With our countrymen, than with foreigners" (Hume 1739/1888, 581). Recent research shows that empathy tends to be biased: First, observers are more empathic to victims who are familiar and similar to themselves than to victims who are different. Second, people are more apt to be empathically aroused by someone's distress in the immediate situation than by distress they know is being experienced by someone elsewhere (Hoffman 1987). But these issues need much more empirical investigation. Cognitive science needs to give us a systematic account of the properties of the empathizing process. What targets and circumstances encourage the initiation of empathy? What variables affect the vividness or strength of empathic feelings? How do empathic feelings combine with other cognitions to influence an agent's conduct? These and other parameters concerning empathy need to be better understood. Moral theory needs to be sensitive, then, to the phenomenon of empathy. The precise impact that the phenomenon should have on moral theory depends on specific properties of empathy—properties that can only be firmly identified and established through psychological research. Thus, moral theory stands to benefit from the work of cognitive science on this topic as well as all the others we have discussed.

Conclusion

This book has canvassed a broad range of philosophical questions and shown how their answers depend partly on work in cognitive science. Answers to some of these questions depend on whether people have the cognitive or psychological resources to satisfy certain desirata. For example, the range of conditions in which people can acquire knowledge or rational belief depends on their perceptual mechanisms and their native strategies for assessing logical and probabilistic relations.

Other philosophical questions address the nature of our understanding of certain basic concepts. For example, ordinary people have a set of mentalistic concepts—a folk psychology—by which they explain and predict their own behavior and the behavior of others. Philosophers are interested in the viability of this folk psychology, but they must first know what it consists in and how it gets deployed. This turns out to be a difficult question that cannot be answered in an "armchair" fashion. Whether the theory theory or the simulation theory is correct, for example, can only be settled with the help of scientific evidence.

Finally, although many questions in philosophy are normative questions (questions of "right" and "wrong"), the correctness of norms sometimes depends on matters of contingent, empirical facts, including psychological facts. In this chapter, I suggested that the correctness or acceptability of ethical norms depends on the feasibility of compliance with those norms given human motivational capacities. This means that if we are to settle certain normative issues, we need answers to questions about human motivational powers. These questions are ones that must be answered by cognitive science.

For many reasons, then, philosophy should work hand in hand with cognitive science, or at least keep tuned to its findings and theories. Philosophy needs to know about the mind, and the mind is a devilishly complex and elusive entity that cannot be well understood at the level philosophy requires without formidable scientific effort. If we are to ply our pursuits as successfully as possible, we need information and insight of the sort that cognitive science can offer.

Suggestions for Further Reading

A brief overview of psychological approaches to concept representation is found in E. E. Smith (1990). Stich (forthcoming) suggests that these kinds of approaches should be reflected in theories of moral concepts. A similar point is urged by Johnson (forthcoming).

Lawrence Kohlberg (1981, 1984) developed a much-discussed "stage" theory of moral-cognitive development. Several philosophers discuss his theory in *Ethics* 92, 3 (April 1982). Gilligan (1982) was triggered partly as a criticism of Kohlberg.

Fiske's hypothesis that four forms of sociality are rooted in innate cognitive structures may not be firmly supported by the evidence, but it is an interesting scheme. See Fiske (1991) or Fiske (in press).

The intriguing research on subjective judgments of well-being is well represented by Schwarz and Strack (1991) and Tversky and Griffin (1991). Expressed preferences may also be constructions that are heavily influenced by elicitation procedures, as discussed by Slovic (1990).

On the psychology of empathy, the best recent anthology is Eisenberg and Strayer (1987). On the role of empathy in morality, see Hoffman (1984, 1987) [R]. The role of moral emotions in our psyche, and their possible evolutionary origins, is discussed by Gibbard (1990). "Ethics and Psychological Realism" is the subtitle of Flanagan (1991) [R], which spells out ways that psychology can enrich moral philosophy.

References

Allport, G. W. (1968). "The Historical Background of Modern Social Psychology," in G. Lindzey and E. Arsonson, eds., *Handbook of Social Psychology,* 2nd ed., vol. 1. Reading, Mass.: Addison-Wesley.

Antell, S. and D. P. Keating (1983). "Perception of Numerical Invariance in Neonates," *Child Development* 54: 695–701.

Astington, J., P. Harris, and D. Olson, eds. (1988). *Developing Theories of Mind.* Cambridge: Cambridge University Press.

Ayer, A. J. (1936). *Language, Truth and Logic.* London: Gollancz.

Bar-Hillel, M. and R. Falk (1982). "Some Teasers Concerning Conditional Probabilities," *Cognition* 11: 109–122.

Barnett, M. A. (1987). "Empathy and Related Responses in Children," in N. Eisenberg and J. Strayer, eds., *Empathy and Its Development.* Cambridge: Cambridge University Press.

Baron-Cohen, S., A. Leslie, and U. Frith (1985). "Does the Autistic Child Have a Theory of Mind?" *Cognition* 21: 37–46.

———. (1986). "Mechanical, Behavioral and Intentional Understanding of Picture Stories in Autistic Children," *British Journal of Developmental Psychology* 4: 113–125.

Barwise, J. and J. Etchemendy (1991). "Visual Information and Valid Reasoning," in W. Zimmerman and S. Cunningham, eds., *Visualization in Teaching and Learning Mathematics* (MAA Notes #19). Washington, D.C.: Mathematical Association of America.

Bavelas, J. B., A. Black, C. R. Lemery, and J. Mullett (1987). "Motor Mimicry as Primitive Empathy," in N. Eisenberg and J. Strayer, eds., *Empathy and Its Development.* Cambridge: Cambridge University Press.

Beakley, B. and P. Ludlow, eds. (1992). *The Philosophy of Mind.* Cambridge, Mass.: MIT Press/Bradford Books.

Bechtel, W. (1988). *Philosophy of Mind.* Hillsdale, N.J.: Lawrence Erlbaum.

Bechtel, W. and A. Abrahamsen (1991). *Connectionism and the Mind.* Oxford: Basil Blackwell.

Berger, S. M. (1962). "Conditioning Through Vicarious Instigation," *Psychological Review* 69: 450–466.

Berkeley, G. (1709). *Essay Toward a New Theory of Vision.* Dublin.

______ . (1713). *Three Dialogues Between Hylas and Philonous.* London.

Biederman, I. (1987). "Recognition-by-Components: A Theory of Human Image Understanding," *Psychological Review* 94: 115–147.

______ . (1990). "Higher-Level Vision," in D. Osherson, S. Kosslyn, and J. Hollerbach, eds., *Visual Cognition and Action.* Cambridge, Mass.: MIT Press/Bradford Books.

Block, N., ed. (1980). *Readings in the Philosophy of Psychology,* vols. 1–2. Cambridge, Mass.: Harvard University Press.

______ . (1981). *Imagery.* Cambridge, Mass.: MIT Press/Bradford Books.

Block, N. (1990). "Inverted Earth," in J. Tomberlin, ed., *Philosophical Perspectives,* vol. 4. Atascadero, Calif.: Ridgeview.

Blum, L. (1980). *Friendship, Altruism, and Morality.* London: Routledge and Kegan Paul.

______ . (1987). "Particularity and Responsiveness," in J. Kagan and S. Lamb, eds., *The Emergence of Morality in Young Children.* Chicago: University of Chicago Press.

Boysen, S. T. and G. G. Berntson (1989) . "Numerical Competence in a Chimpanzee," *Pan Troglodytes: Journal of Comparative Psychology* 103: 23–31.

Brickman, P. (1975). "Adaptation Level Determinants of Satisfaction with Equal and Unequal Outcome Distributions in Skill and Chance Situations," *Journal of Personality and Social Psychology* 32: 191–198.

Brickman, P. and D. T. Campbell (1971). "Hedonic Relativism and Planning the Good Society," in M. H. Appley, ed., *Adaptation Level Theory.* New York: Academic Press.

Butterworth, G. E. (1991). "The Ontogeny and Phylogeny of Joint Visual Attention," in A. Whiten, ed., *Natural Theories of Mind.* Oxford: Basil Blackwell.

Butterworth, G. E. and E. Cochran (1980). "Towards a Mechanism of Joint Visual Attention in Human Infancy," *International Journal of Behavioral Development* 19: 253–272.

Campbell, A. (1981). *The Sense of Well-Being in America.* New York: McGraw-Hill.

Carey, S. (1985). *Conceptual Change in Childhood.* Cambridge, Mass.: MIT Press/Bradford Books.

Cherniak, C. (1986). *Minimal Rationality.* Cambridge, Mass.: MIT Press/Bradford Books.

Churchland, P. M. (1979). *Scientific Realism and the Plasticity of Mind.* Cambridge: Cambridge University Press.

______ . (1981). "Eliminative Materialism and the Propositional Attitudes," *The Journal of Philosophy* 78: 67–90.

______ . (1988a). "Perceptual Plasticity and Theoretical Neutrality: A Reply to Jerry Fodor," *Philosophy of Science* 55: 167–187.

______ . (1988b). *Matter and Consciousness,* revised edition. Cambridge, Mass.: MIT Press/Bradford Books.

______ . (1989). *A Neurocomputational Perspective.* Cambridge, Mass.: MIT Press/Bradford Books.

Churchland, P. S. (1980). "Language, Thought, and Information Processing," *Nous* 14: 147–170.

______ . (1986). *Neurophilosophy.* Cambridge, Mass.: MIT Press/Bradford Books.

Clark, A. (1989). *Microcognition: Philosophy, Cognitive Science, and Parallel Distributed Processings.* Cambridge, Mass.: MIT Press/Bradford Books.

Cohen, L. J. (1981). "Can Human Irrationality Be Experimentally Demonstrated?" *Behavioral and Brain Sciences* 4: 317–370.

Cummins, R. (1989). *Meaning and Mental Representation.* Cambridge, Mass.: MIT Press/Bradford Books.

Darwin, C. (1872/1955). *The Expression of the Emotions in Man and Animals.* New York: Philosophical Library.

Davidson, D. (1984). *Inquiries into Truth and Interpretation.* Oxford: Clarendon Press.

Davies, M. and T. Stone, eds. (1993). *Mental Simulation: Philosophical and Psychological Essays.* Oxford: Basil Blackwell.

Davis, H. and S. A. Bradford (1986). "Counting Behavior by Rats in a Simulated Natural Environment," *Ethology* 73: 265–280.

Dennett, D. C. (1978). *Brainstorms.* Montgomery, Vt.: Bradford Books.

______ . (1986). "The Logical Geography of Computational Approaches: A View from the East Pole," in R. Harnish and M. Brand, eds., *The Representation of Knowledge and Belief.* Tucson: University of Arizona Press.

______ . (1987). *The Intentional Stance.* Cambridge, Mass.: MIT Press/Bradford Books.

______ . (1991). *Consciousness Explained.* Boston: Little, Brown and Co.

Descartes, R. (1637). *Discourse on Method.* Leiden: Maire.

Dretske, F. (1981). *Knowledge and the Flow of Information.* Cambridge, Mass.: MIT Press/Bradford Books.

______ . (1988). *Explaining Behavior.* Cambridge, Mass.: MIT Press/Bradford Books.

Easterlin, R. A. (1974). "Does Economic Growth Improve the Human Lot? Some Empirical Evidence," in P. A. David and M. W. Reder, eds., *Nations and Households in Economic Growth.* New York: Academic Press.

Eisenberg, N. and R. A. Fabes (1990). "Empathy: Conceptualization, Assessment, and Relation to Prosocial Behavior, " *Motivation and Emotion* 14: 131–149.

Eisenberg, N. and R. Lennon (1983). "Sex Differences in Empathy and Related Capacities," *Psychological Bulletin* 94: 100–131.

Eisenberg, N. and J. Strayer, eds. (1987). *Empathy and Its Development.* Cambridge: Cambridge University Press.

Enc, B. (1986). "Essentialism Without Individual Essences: Causation, Kinds, Supervenience, and Restricted Identities," in P. French, T. Uehling, and H. Wettstein, eds., *Midwest Studies in Philosophy,* vol. 11. Minneapolis: University of Minnesota Press.

Estes, W. (1986). "Array Models for Category Learning," *Cognitive Psychology* 18: 500–549.

Fantz, R. L. (1961). "The Origin of Form Perception," *Scientific American* 204: 66–72.

Feldman, R. (1988). "Having Evidence," in D. Austin, ed., *Philosophical Analysis.* Dordrecht: Kluwer Academic Publishers.

Finke, R. A. and R. N. Shepard (1986). "Visual Functions of Mental Imagery," in K. R. Boff, L. Kaufman, and J. P. Thomas, eds.,

Handbook of Perception and Human Performance. New York: Wiley.

Fiske, A. P. (1991). *Structures of Social Life: The Four Elementary Forms of Human Relations.* New York: Free Press.

______ . (in press). "Four Elementary Forms of Sociality: Framework for a Unified Theory of Social Relations," *Psychological Review.*

Flanagan, O. (1991). *Varieties of Moral Personality: Ethics and Psychological Realism.* Cambridge, Mass.: Harvard University Press.

______ . (1992). *Consciousness Reconsidered.* Cambridge, Mass.: MIT Press/Bradford Books.

Fodor, J. A. (1968). *Psychological Explanation.* New York: Random House.

______ . (1975). *The Language of Thought.* New York: Thomas Crowell.

______ . (1981). *Representations.* Cambridge, Mass.: MIT Press/Bradford Books.

______ . (1983). *Modularity of Mind.* Cambridge, Mass.: MIT Press/Bradford Books.

______ . (1984). "Observation Reconsidered," *Philosophy of Science* 51: 23–43.

______ . (1987). *Psychosemantics.* Cambridge, Mass.: MIT Press/Bradford Books.

______ . (1988). "A Reply to Churchland's 'Perceptual Plasticity and Theoretical Neutrality'," *Philosophy of Science* 55: 188–198.

______ . (1990). *A Theory of Content and Other Essays.* Cambridge, Mass.: MIT Press/Bradford Books.

Fodor, J. A. and Z. Pylyshyn (1988). "Connectionism and Cognitive Architecture: A Critical Analysis," *Cognition* 28: 3–71.

Fuentes, C. (1964). *The Death of Artemio Cruz.* New York: Farrar Straus Giroux.

Gelman, R. and C. R. Gallistel (1978). *The Child's Understanding of Number.* Cambridge, Mass.: Harvard University Press.

Gelman, R. and J. G. Greeno (1989). "On the Nature of Competence: Principles for Understanding in a Domain," in L. B. Resnick, ed., *Knowing and Learning: Issues for a Cognitive Science of Instruction.* Hillsdale, N.J.: Lawrence Erlbaum.

Gelman, S. and H. Wellman (1991). "Insides and Essences: Early Understanding of the Non-Obvious," *Cognition* 38: 213–244.

Gibbard, A. (1990). *Wise Choices, Apt Feelings.* Cambridge, Mass.: Harvard University Press.

Giere, R. (1988). *Explaining Science.* Chicago: University of Chicago Press.

Gigerenzer, G., W. Hell, and H. Blank (1988). "Presentation and Content: The Use of Base Rates as a Continuous Variable," *Journal of Experimental Psychology: Human Perception and Performance* 14: 513–525.

Gilligan, C. (1982). *In a Different Voice.* Cambridge, Mass.: Harvard University Press.

Gleitman, H. (1981). *Psychology.* New York: W. W. Norton.

Goldman, A. I. (1979). "What Is Justified Belief?" in G. Pappas, ed., *Justification and Knowledge.* Dordrecht: D. Reidel. Reprinted in Goldman (1992a).

______ . (1986). *Epistemology and Cognition.* Cambridge, Mass.: Harvard University Press.

______ . (1989). "Interpretation Psychologized," *Mind and Language* 4: 161–185. Reprinted in Goldman (1992a) and in Davies and Stone (1993).

______ . (1992a). *Liaisons: Philosophy Meets the Cognitive and Social Sciences.* Cambridge, Mass.: MIT Press/Bradford Books.

______ . (1992b). "Epistemic Folkways and Scientific Epistemology," in Goldman (1992a).

______ . (1992c). "In Defense of the Simulation Theory," *Mind and Language* 7: 104–119. Reprinted in Davies and Stone (1993).

______ . (1992d). "Empathy, Mind, and Morals," *Proceedings and Addresses of the American Philosophical Association.* Reprinted in Davies and Stone (1993).

______ . (1993a). "The Psychology of Folk Psychology," *Behavioral and Brain Sciences* 16: 15–28.

______ . ed. (1993b). *Readings in Philosophy and Cognitive Science.* Cambridge, Mass.: MIT Press/Bradford Books.

Goodman, N. (1978). *Ways of Worldmaking.* Indianapolis: Hackett Publishing Company.

Gopnik, A. (1993). "How We Know Our Minds: The Illusion of First-Person Knowledge of Intentionality," *Behavioral and Brain Sciences* 16.

Gordon, R. M. (1986). "Folk Psychology as Simulation," *Mind and Language* 1: 158–171.

______ . (1992). "The Simulation Theory: Objections and Misconceptions," *Mind and Language* 7: 11–34.

Greenwald, A. (1980). "The Totalitarian Ego: Fabrication and Revision of Personal History," *American Psychologist* 35: 603–618.

Gruber, J. S. (1965). *Studies in Lexical Relations.* Doctoral dissertation, MIT. Reprinted (1976) as part of *Lexical Structures in Syntax and Semantics.* Amsterdam: North-Holland.

Haan, N. (1975). "Hypothetical and Actual Moral Reasoning in a Situation of Civil Disobedience," *Journal of Personality and Social Psychology* 32: 255–270.

Hanson, N. R. (1958). *Patterns of Discovery.* Cambridge: Cambridge University Press.

Hardin, C. L. (1988). *Color for Philosophers.* Indianapolis: Hackett Publishing Company.

Harman, G. (1990). "The Intrinsic Quality of Experience, " in J. Tomberlin, ed., *Philosophical Perspectives,* vol. 4. Atascadero, Calif.: Ridgeview.

Harris, P. L. (1989). *Children and Emotion: The Development of Psychological Understanding.* Oxford: Basil Blackwell.

______ . (1992). "From Simulation to Folk Psychology: The Case for Development," *Mind and Language* 7: 120–144.

Hilbert, D. R. (1987). *Color and Color Perception.* Stanford: Center for the Study of Language and Information.

Hirsch, E. (1982). *The Concept of Identity.* New York: Oxford University Press.

Hoffman, M. L. (1984). "Empathy, Its Limitations and Its Role in a Comprehensive Moral Theory," in W. Kurtines and J. Gewirtz, eds., *Morality, Moral Behavior and Moral Development.* New York: John Wiley.

______ . (1987). "The Contribution of Empathy to Justice and Moral Judgment," in N. Eisenberg and J. Strayer, eds.,

Empathy and Its Development. Cambridge: Cambridge University Press.

Holland, J., K. Holyoak, R. Nisbett, and P. Thagard (1986). *Induction: Processes of Inference, Learning, and Discovery.* Cambridge, Mass.: MIT Press/Bradford Books.

Holstein, C. (1976). "Development of Moral Judgment: A Longitudinal Study," *Child Development* 47: 51–61.

Horgan, T. and J. Tienson, eds. (1991). *Connectionism and the Philosophy of Mind.* Dordrecht: Kluwer Academic Publishers.

Hull, C. L. (1933). *Hypnosis and Suggestibility.* New York: Appleton-Century.

Hume, D. (1739/1888). *A Treatise of Human Nature,* L. Selby-Bigge, ed. Oxford: Clarendon Press.

Hurvich, L. M. and D. Jameson (1957). "An Opponent-Process Theory of Color Vision," *Psychological Review* 64: 384–404.

Jackendoff, R. (1983). *Semantics and Cognition.* Cambridge, Mass.: MIT Press/Bradford Books.

______ . (1987). *Consciousness and the Computational Mind.* Cambridge, Mass.: MIT Press/Bradford Books.

______ . (1990). *Semantic Structures.* Cambridge, Mass.: MIT Press/Bradford Books.

Johnson, M. (forthcoming). *Moral Imagination: Implications of Cognitive Science for Ethics.* Chicago: University of Chicago Press.

Johnson-Laird, P. N. and R.M.J. Byrne (1990). "Meta-Logical Problems: Knights, Knaves, and Rips," *Cognition* 36: 69–84.

______ . (1991). *Deduction.* Hove: Erlbaum.

Kahneman, D., P. Slovic, and A. Tversky, eds. (1982). *Judgment Under Uncertainty: Heuristics and Biases.* Cambridge: Cambridge University Press.

Kahneman, D. and A. Tversky (1973). "On the Psychology of Prediction," *Psychological Review* 80: 237–251.

Kant, I. (1787/1965). *The Critique of Pure Reason,* 2nd ed. Translated by N. Kemp Smith. London: MacMillan.

Keil, F. (1989). *Concepts, Kinds, and Cognitive Development.* Cambridge, Mass.: MIT Press/Bradford Books.

Kellman, P. J. and E. S. Spelke (1983). "Perception of Partly Occluded Objects in Infancy," *Cognitive Psychology* 15: 483–524.

Kitcher, P. (1983). *The Nature of Mathematical Knowledge.* Oxford: Oxford University Press.

______ . (1985). *Vaulting Ambition: Sociobiology and the Quest for Human Nature.* Cambridge, Mass.: MIT Press.

______ . (1988). "Mathematical Naturalism," in W. Aspray and P. Kitcher, eds., *History and Philosophy of Modern Mathematics.* Minneapolis: University of Minnesota Press.

Klinnert, M. (1981). "Infants' Use of Mothers' Facial Expressions for Regulating Their Own Behavior." Paper presented to the meeting of the Society for Research in Child Development, Boston.

Kohlberg, L. (1981). *Essays on Moral Development.* Vol. 1, *The Philosophy of Moral Development.* New York: Harper & Row.

______ . (1984). *Essays on Moral Development.* Vol. 2, *The Psychology of Moral Development.* New York: Harper & Row.

Kornblith, H. (1993). *Inductive Inference and Its Natural Ground.* Cambridge, Mass.: MIT Press/Bradford Books.

Kosslyn, S. M. (1980). *Image and Mind.* Cambridge, Mass.: Harvard University Press.

______ . (1990). "Mental Imagery," in D. N. Osherson, S. M. Kosslyn, and J. M. Hollerbach, eds., *Visual Cognition and Action.* Cambridge, Mass.: MIT Press/Bradford Books.

Krebs, D. L. (1975). "Empathy and Altruism," *Journal of Personality and Social Psychology* 32: 1134–1146.

Kripke, S. A. (1972). "Naming and Necessity," in D. Davidson and G. Harman, eds., *Semantics of Natural Language.* Dordrecht: D. Reidel.

Kuhn, T. (1962). *The Structure of Scientific Revolutions.* Chicago: University of Chicago Press.

Lakatos, I. (1970). "Falsification and the Methodology of Scientific Research Programmes," in I. Lakatos and A. Musgrave, eds., *Criticism and the Growth of Knowledge.* Cambridge: Cambridge University Press.

Lakoff, G. (1987). *Women, Fire, and Dangerous Things.* Chicago: University of Chicago Press.

Lakoff, G. and M. Johnson (1980). *Metaphors We Live By.* Chicago: University of Chicago Press.

Land, E. (1977). "The Retinex Theory of Color Vision," *Scientific American* 237: 108–128.

Langley, P., H. Simon, G. Bradshaw, and J. Zytkow (1987). *Scientific Discovery.* Cambridge, Mass.: MIT Press.

Lennon, R. and N. Eisenberg (1987). "Gender and Age Differences in Empathy and Sympathy," in N. Eisenberg and J. Strayer, eds., *Empathy and Its Development.* Cambridge: Cambridge University Press.

Leslie, A. (1987). "Pretense and Representation: The Origins of 'Theory of Mind'," *Psychological Review* 94: 412–426.

Lewis, D. K. (1966). "An Argument for the Identity Theory," *The Journal of Philosophy* 63: 17–25.

Locke, J. (1694). *Essay Concerning Human Understanding,* 2nd ed.

Lycan, W. (1987). *Consciousness.* Cambridge, Mass.: MIT Press/ Bradford Books.

——— , ed. (1990). *Mind and Cognition.* Oxford: Basil Blackwell.

Macnamara, J. (1986). *A Border Dispute.* Cambridge, Mass.: MIT Press/Bradford Books.

Markman, E. (1989). *Categorization and Naming in Children.* Cambridge, Mass.: MIT Press/Bradford Books.

Marr, D. (1982). *Vision.* San Francisco: W. H. Freeman.

McDougall, W. (1908). *Introduction to Social Psychology.* London: Methuen.

McGinn, C. (1989). *Mental Content.* Oxford: Basil Blackwell.

Mead, G. H. (1934). *Mind, Self, and Society.* Chicago: University of Chicago Press.

Meck, W. H. and R. M. Church (1983). "A Mode Control Model of Counting and Timing Processes," *Journal of Experimental Psychology: Animal Behavior Processes* 9: 320–334.

Medin, D. and M. Schaffer (1978). "A Context Theory of Classification Learning," *Psychological Review* 85: 207–238.

Mill, J. S. (1843/1881). *A System of Logic,* 8th ed. New York.

Millikan R. (1984). *Language, Thought, and Other Biological Categories.* Cambridge, Mass.: MIT Press/Bradford Books.

Nisbett, R., D. Krantz, C. Jepson, and Z. Kunda (1983). "The Use of Statistical Heuristics in Everyday Inductive Reasoning," *Psychological Review* 90: 339–363.

Nisbett, R. and L. Ross (1980). *Human Inference: Strategies and Shortcomings of Social Judgment.* Englewood Cliffs, N.J.: Prentice-Hall.

Osherson, D. N. (1990). "Judgment," in D. N. Osherson and E. E. Smith, eds., *Thinking.* Cambridge, Mass.: MIT Press/Bradford Books.

O'Toole, R. and R. Dubin (1968). "Baby Feeding and Body Sway: An Experiment in George Herbert Mead's 'Taking the Role of the Other'," *Journal of Personality and Social Psychology* 10: 59–65.

Pastore, N. (1961). "Number Sense and 'Counting' Ability in the Canary," *Zeitschrift für Tierpsychologie* 18: 561–573.

Perner, J. (1991). *Understanding the Representational Mind.* Cambridge, Mass.: MIT Press/Bradford Books.

Pinker, S., ed. (1985). *Visual Cognition.* Cambridge, Mass.: MIT Press/Bradford Books.

Plato (1937). *The Dialogues of Plato,* vol. 1. Translated by B. Jowett. New York: Random House.

Pollock, J. (1989). *How to Build a Person.* Cambridge, Mass.: MIT Press/Bradford Books.

Potter, M. (1990). "Remembering," in D. Osherson and E. E. Smith, eds., *Thinking.* Cambridge, Mass.: MIT Press/Bradford Books.

Putnam, H. (1963). "Brains and Behavior," in R. Butler, ed., *Analytical Philosophy, Second Series.* Oxford: Basil Blackwell.

______ . (1967). "Psychological Predicates," in W. H. Capitan and D. D. Merrill, eds., *Art, Mind, and Religion.* Pittsburgh: University of Pittsburgh Press.

______ . (1975). "The Meaning of 'Meaning'," in K. Gunderson, ed., *Language, Mind, and Knowledge.* Minneapolis: University of Minnesota Press.

Quine, W. V. (1960). *Word and Object.* Cambridge, Mass.: MIT Press.

______ . (1969). "Epistemology Naturalized," in *Ontological Relativity and Other Essays.* New York: Columbia University Press.

______ . (1973). *The Roots of Reference.* La Salle, Ill.: Open Court.

Rawls, J. (1971). *A Theory of Justice.* Cambridge, Mass.: Harvard University Press.

Rips, L. J. (1989). "The Psychology of Knights and Knaves," *Cognition* 31: 85–116.

Rips, L. J. and S. L. Marcus (1977). "Supposition and the Analysis of Conditional Sentences," in M. Just and P. Carpenter, eds., *Cognitive Processes in Comprehension.* Hillsdale, N.J.: Lawrence Erlbaum.

Rosenthal, D., ed. (1991). *The Nature of Mind.* Oxford: Oxford University Press.

Schiffer, S. (1987). *Remnants of Meaning.* Cambridge, Mass.: MIT Press/Bradford Books.

Schopenhauer, A. (1841/1965). *On the Basis of Morality.* Translated by E.F.J. Payne. Indianapolis: Bobbs-Merrill.

Schwarz, N. and F. Strack (1991). "Evaluating One's Life: A Judgment Model of Subjective Well-Being," in F. Strack, M. Argyle, and N. Schwarz, eds., *Subjective Well-Being.* Oxford: Pergamon Press.

Searle, J. (1983). *Intentionality.* Cambridge: Cambridge University Press.

______ . (1992). *The Rediscovery of the Mind.* Cambridge, Mass.: MIT Press/Bradford Books.

Shepard, R. N. and L. A. Cooper (1982). *Mental Images and Their Transformations.* Cambridge, Mass.: MIT Press/Bradford Books.

Simner, M. L. (1971). "Newborn's Response to the Cry of Another Infant," *Developmental Psychology* 5: 136–150.

Slovic, P. (1990). "Choice," in D. Osherson and E. Smith, eds., *Thinking.* Cambridge, Mass.: MIT Press/Bradford Books.

Smith, A. (1759/1976). *The Theory of Moral Sentiments.* Oxford: Oxford University Press.

Smith, E. E. (1990). "Categorization," in D. N. Osherson and E. E. Smith, eds., *Thinking.* Cambridge, Mass.: MIT Press/Bradford Books.

Smith, E. E. and D. L. Medin (1981). *Categories and Concepts.* Cambridge, Mass.: Harvard University Press.

Smolensky, P. (1988). "On the Proper Treatment of Connectionism," *Behavioral and Brain Sciences* 11: 1–74.

Smullyan, R. (1978). *What Is the Name of This Book? The Riddle of Dracula and Other Logical Puzzles.* Englewood Cliffs, N.J.: Prentice-Hall.

Soja, N., S. Carey, and E. Spelke (1991). "Ontological Categories Guide Young Children's Inductions of Word Meaning: Object Terms and Substance Terms," *Cognition* 38: 179–211.

Spelke, E. S. (1990a). "Origins of Visual Knowledge," in D. N. Osherson, S. M. Kosslyn, and J. M. Hollerbach, eds., *Visual Cognition and Action.* Cambridge, Mass.: MIT Press/Bradford Books.

______ . (1990b). "Principles of Object Perception," *Cognitive Science* 14: 29–56.

Spencer, H. (1870). *The Principles of Psychology,* 2nd ed., vol. 1. London: Williams and Norgate.

Starkey, P. and R. G. Cooper (1980). "Perception of Numbers by Human Infants," *Science* 210: 1033–1035.

Starkey, P., E. Spelke, and R. Gelman (1983). "Detection of Intermodal Numerical Correspondence by Human Infants," *Science* 222: 179–181.

______ . (1990). "Numerical Abstraction by Human Infants," *Cognition* 36: 97–128.

Sterelny, K. (1990). *The Representational Theory of Mind.* Oxford: Basil Blackwell.

Stich, S. P. (1983). *From Folk Psychology to Cognitive Science.* Cambridge, Mass.: MIT Press/Bradford Books

______ . (1990). "Rationality," in D. Osherson and E. Smith, eds., *Thinking.* Cambridge, Mass.: MIT Press.

______ . (forthcoming). "Moral Philosophy and Mental Representation," in M. Hechter, L. Nadel, and R. Michod, eds., *The Origin of Values.* Hawthorne, N.Y.: Aldine de Gruyter.

Stich, S. P. and S. Nichols (1992). "Folk Psychology: Simulation or Tacit Theory?" *Mind and Language* 7: 35–71.

Stipek, D. J. (1984). "Young Children's Performance Expectations: Logical Analysis or Wishful Thinking?" in I. Nicholls, ed., *Advances in Motivation and Achievement,* vol. 3. Greenwich, Conn.: JAI Press.

Stotland, E. (1969). "Exploratory Studies of Empathy," in L. Berkowitz, ed., *Advances in Experimental Social Psychology,* vol. 4. New York: Academic Press.

Strack, F., N. Schwarz, and E. Gschneidinger (1985). "Happiness and Reminiscing: The Role of Time Perspective, Mood, and

Mode of Thinking," *Journal of Personality and Social Psychology* 49: 1460–1469.

Streri, A. and E. S. Spelke (1988). "Haptic Perception of Objects in Infancy," *Cognitive Psychology* 20: 1–23.

Talmy, L. (1988). "Force Dynamics in Language and Cognition," *Cognitive Science* 12: 49–100.

Taylor, S. E. (1989). *Positive Illusions: Creative Self-Deception and the Healthy Mind.* New York: Basic Books.

Thagard, P. (1989). "Explanatory Coherence," *Behavioral and Brain Sciences* 12: 435–467.

______ . (1992). *Conceptual Revolutions.* Princeton: Princeton University Press.

Thompson, E., A. Palacios, and F. Varela (1992). "Ways of Coloring," *Behavioral and Brain Sciences* 15: 1–74.

Thompson, R. A. (1987). "Empathy and Emotional Understanding: The Early Development of Empathy," in N. Eisenberg and J. Strayer, eds., *Empathy and Its Development.* Cambridge: Cambridge University Press.

Turing, A. M. (1950). "Computing Machinery and Intelligence," *Mind* 59: 433–460.

Tversky, A. and D. Griffin (1991). "Endowment and Contrast in Judgments of Well-Being," in F. Strack, M. Argyle, and N. Schwarz, eds., *Subjective Well-Being.* Oxford: Pergamon Press.

Tversky, A. and D. Kahneman (1983). "Extensional Versus Intuitive Reasoning: The Conjunctive Fallacy in Probability Judgment," *Psychological Review* 90: 292–315.

Tye, M. (1991). *The Imagery Debate.* Cambridge, Mass.: MIT Press/ Bradford Books.

Van den Berghe, P. (1983). "Human Inbreeding Avoidance: Culture in Nature," *Behavioral and Brain Sciences* 6: 91–123.

Walker, L. (1984). "Sex Differences in the Development of Moral Reasoning: A Critical Review," *Child Development* 55: 677–691.

Walker, L., B. DeVries, and S. Trevethan (1987). "Moral Stages and Moral Orientations in Real-Life and Hypothetical Dilemmas," *Child Development* 58: 842–858.

Wallach, H. and D. O'Connell (1953). "The Kinetic Depth Effect," *Journal of Experimental Psychology* 45: 205–217.

Wellman, H. (1990). *The Child's Theory of Mind.* Cambridge, Mass.: MIT Press/Bradford Books.

Wertheimer, M. (1923). "Principles of Perceptual Organization," *Psychologische Forschungen* 4: 301–350.

Wimmer, H. and J. Perner (1983). "Beliefs About Beliefs: Representation and Constraining Function of Wrong Beliefs in Children's Understanding of Deception," *Cognition* 13: 103–128.

Wittgenstein, L. (1953). *Philosophical Investigations.* New York: MacMillan.

Wynn, K. (1992a). "Addition and Subtraction by Human Infants," *Nature* 358: 749–750.

______ . (1992b). "Evidence Against Empiricist Accounts of the Origins of Numerical Knowledge," *Mind and Language* 7.

About the Book and Author

One of the most fruitful interdisciplinary boundaries in contemporary scholarship is that between philosophy and cognitive science. Now that solid empirical results about the activities of the human mind are available, it is no longer necessary for philosophers to practice armchair psychology.

In this short, accessible, and entertaining book, Alvin Goldman presents a masterly survey of recent work in cognitive science that has particular relevance to philosophy. Besides providing a valuable review of the most suggestive work in cognitive and social psychology, Goldman demonstrates conclusively that the best work in philosophy in a surprising number of different fields—including philosophy of science, epistemology, metaphysics, and ethics as well as philosophy of mind—must take into account empirical breakthroughs in psychology.

One of those rare texts that will also be useful for professionals, *Philosophical Applications of Cognitive Science* is appropriate for students in a wide range of philosophy courses. It will also interest researchers and students in psychology who are intrigued by the wider theoretical implications of their work.

Alvin I. Goldman is professor of philosophy and research scientist in cognitive science at the University of Arizona. He is the author of *A Theory of Human Action*, *Epistemology and Cognition*, and *Liaisons: Philosophy Meets the Cognitive and Social Sciences* as well as many articles on philosophy and cognitive science.

Index